... Scrooge was better than his word ... it was always said of him, that he knew how to keep Christmas well ... May that be truly said of us, and all of us!

— CHARLES DICKENS, *A Christmas Carol*

1879,
A. HOWS

The nights are wholesome, then no planets strike,
No fairy takes, nor witch hath power to charm,
So hallow'd and so gracious is the time. ...

—Act 1 Scene 1 *Hamlet*,
Marcellus describes the Season of Christmas.

Keeping Christmas Well

— Until (at least) January 6th

by Artemesia D'Ecca

Essential Facts about the Season of Christmas

A Phaëton Guide

PHAETON
PUBLISHING LTD.
Dublin

— Keeping Christmas Well —

FIRST PUBLISHED IN THE U.K. & IRELAND 2011
PHAETON PUBLISHING LIMITED, DUBLIN

Copyright © Artemesia D'Ecca 2011
Artemesia D'Ecca has asserted her right
to be identified as the author of this work

Cover, jacket & design of book (& of eBook)
© O'Dwyer & Jones Design Partnership 2011

Printed and bound in the United Kingdom
by MPG Biddles Ltd., King's Lynn

ISBN: 978-1-908420-00-8 (HARDBACK)

*British Library Cataloguing In Publication
Data: A catalogue record for this book
is available from the British Library.*

THE SAME BOOK CONTENT ALSO AVAILABLE IN
ISBN: 978-1-908420-02-2 (PDF EBOOK)
WITH ALL IMAGES OPTIMIZED FOR EREADERS
The PDF-format eBook and its images are designed specifically to suit current black+white (e-ink) e-readers–*Amazon Kindle* and *Sony Reader*, etc.

All rights reserved. No part of this publication may be reproduced, stored in, or introduced into a retrieval system, or transmitted, or copied in any form or by any means (electronic, digital, mechanical, photocopying, recording or otherwise) without the prior permission of the publisher.

This book is sold subject to the condition that it shall not, by way of trade or otherwise, be lent, re-sold, hired out or otherwise circulated, without the publisher's prior consent in any form of binding or cover other than that in which it is published, and with a similar condition imposed on all subsequent purchasers.

WWW.PHAETON.IE

V

THE NATIVITY
(*BOOK OF HOURS*,
NORTHERN FRANCE,
15th CENTURY)

Keeping Christmas Well

CONTENTS

Part I
PAGE

Some Makers & Milestones of Christmas
—a personal selection—

i.	Charles Dickens & Washington Irving	2
ii.	Robert Seymour	9
iii.	Pagan Rome & its Empire	11
iv.	Saint Nicholas	12
v.	Saint Francis of Assisi	19
vi.	Martin Luther	21
vii.	Marchmount Nedham, England, 1600s	22
viii.	Edmund Andros, New England, 1600s	24
ix.	Henry Livingston Jr. & Clement C. Moore & Don Foster	25
x.	*The Children's Friend*, 1821	31
xi.	Prince Albert & Mr Mike Carr	33
xii.	Thomas Nast	37
xiii.	Ulysses S. Grant	39
xiv.	Valentine Davies	39
xv.	Col. Harry Shoup, USAF	39
xvi.	The Year 1958	40
xvii.	Unknown author of *Dán d'Oidhche Nodlag*	41

Continued

Keeping Christmas Well

Contents

Part II   page

A Question-&-Answer Guide to the Season of Christmas

Chapter 1	The Merry Christmas —Where it Came From	43
Chapter 2	*Christmas Calendar:* The 40 Days of Christmas	60
Chapter 3	*Interlude:* The Tom & Jerry	74
Chapter 4	*Christmas Calendar:* The 12 Days of Christmas	78
Chapter 5	*Interlude:* Scrooge Movies	92
Chapter 6	*Christmas Calendar:* The 20 Days of Christmas	108
Chapter 7	*Interlude:* Christmas Movies	137
Chapter 8	The Vigils of Christmas	147
Chapter 9	The Banning of Christmas	157
Chapter 10	*Interlude:* More Christmas Movies	186
Chapter 11	The Resurgent Christmas of the English-speaking World	199
Chapter 12	The Street Carnival	216
Chapter 13	Other Days & Seasons	236
Chapter 14	*Afters:* Notes on 4 Christmas foods	247
	Christmas Cookies	256
	A Visit from St Nicholas, 1823	264
Sources		266

'CHRISTMAS EVE' – DELIVERY OF CHILDREN'S GIFTS
(LUDWIG RICHTER, DRESDEN, C. 1830)

PART I

MAKERS & MILESTONES OF CHRISTMAS

Ollowing is a short Honour Roll of People and Cultures that have shaped, defended, or enriched

Two Writers, and an Artist—

Keeping Christmas Well

1. **Charles Dickens** (1812–1870) and **Washington Irving** (1783–1859) come first in this list because, without their combined efforts—in particular, the pioneering work of Irving—much of the world might be without a Christmas today.

CHARLES DICKENS IN 1842
(*PORTRAIT:* F. ALEXANDER)

Both men wrote in the first half of the 19th century, when English-speaking countries were turning their backs on Christmas. Many in England had stopped celebrating the holiday; many in the U.S. had *never* celebrated it; and powerful forces in both countries were determined that Christmas should remain an ordinary working day.

WASHINGTON IRVING *C.*1820

In England, the near-death of Christmas was remarkable, in view of the wild exuberance with which Christmas—'Old Christmas,' as it would later be called—traditionally had been celebrated there. Old Christmas (which retained its full vigour until the second half of the

(R. SEYMOUR, *THE BOOK OF CHRISTMAS*, 1836)

17th century) started at Halloween with the appointment of Lords of Misrule. The position of Lord of Misrule was prestigious, often highly paid, and usually held by someone of high rank. Strange or wonderful as it now seems, the duty of the Lord of Misrule was to ensure that anarchy reigned for three months, as Christmas did not end until February. Part of the job of the Lord of Misrule was the wearing of a fanciful ruffed costume (as shown right) often made of the costliest materials.

'THE LORD OF MISRULE' (1836, *THE BOOK OF CHRISTMAS*, R. SEYMOUR)

Masquerade and street theatre were part of the 'Old Christmas,' and the amount of food consumed was legendary: *'He is busier than the ovens in England at Christmas,'* is a translation of an old Italian proverb.

This style of Christmas celebration flourished for about a thousand years, but by the Victorian era, it had vanished and was being commemorated as exotic history, sometimes with a note of disapproval at the idea of 'a feast of meat and drink' being sustained for twelve days. The

'CHRISTMAS PUDDING' (R. SEYMOUR, 1836)

3

Part 1

Makers & Milestones of Christmas

4
Keeping Christmas Well

ENGLAND'S 'OLD CHRISTMAS' (IN PARTICULAR THE PROFUSION OF FOOD AND DRINK) PERSONIFIED AS THE CHILDREN OF CHRISTMAS,

—*THE BOOK OF CHRISTMAS*, FRONTISPIECE, DRAWN & ENGRAVED BY ROBERT SEYMOUR, LONDON, 1836.

19th century celebration of Christmas in England had grown staid, private, and almost depressing, if the following 1862 entry in *Chambers's Encyclopaedia* is anything to go by:

> But within the last hundred years, the festivities once appropriate to Christmas have much fallen off. These at one time lasted with more or less brilliancy till Candlemas, and with great spirit till Twelfth Day; but now a meeting in the evening, composed when possible, of the various branches of the family, is all that distinguishes the day above others.

'CHRISTMAS MORNING—THREE GENERATIONS' (*ILLUSTRATED LONDON NEWS* [*I.L.N.*], 1883)

In America, at the same time, there was no

consistency to the celebration of Christmas. Many in New England disapproved of it and ignored it; and in New York, everything to do with Christmas was extreme: whether for good—notably, our modern Santa Claus, created in New York; or for bad—in particular the riots to which the season gave rise.

(L.PRANG ED., 1864)

Part 1

Makers & Milestones of Christmas

ST PETER'S, BARCLAY ST. NEW YORK, 1831

In 1806, a mob gathered outside New York City's only Catholic church, St Peter's, inside which a Midnight Mass was underway. The street fighting that followed led to the first death-in-service of a New York City law-enforcement officer. In 1827, the city suffered a major New Year's riot, driven, it seems, by class differences. The year before, even cadets at West Point, in New York State, fell victim to the rioting culture, their determination to celebrate Christmas with alcohol resulting in the famous 'Eggnog Riot' of 1826.

It started with a Christmas Eve party, for which some cadets had smuggled in rum and whiskey. In the course of a drunken night and morning, shots were fired, property was damaged, and some officers were assaulted. A court-martial followed and eleven cadets were expelled. The rum had come from a nearby tavern famous for its eggnog: Benny Havens's. This legendary haunt

BENNY HAVENS'S TAVERN IN 1839 - DETAIL FROM PANEL PAINTED IN 1939 BY PAUL C. MᶜELROY (FOR WEST POINT ARMY MESS): BENNY HAVENS, TO LEFT, HOLDS THE FLAGON FOR MIXING HIS EGGNOG ('HOT FLIP') AND THE RED-HOT POKER FOR HEATING IT. THE OFFICER HOLDING QUILL AND PAPER IS LT. LUCIUS O'BRIEN WHO WROTE A POETIC TRIBUTE TO BENNY HAVENS, WHICH, SUNG TO THE TUNE OF THE IRISH REBEL SONG *THE WEARING OF THE GREEN*, REMAINS A FAVOURITE AT WEST POINT TODAY.

Keeping Christmas Well

was officially out-of-bounds to cadets, but nevertheless the favourite of many [>]. Ex-West-Point Cadet Edgar Allan Poe wrote that Old Ben [Havens] was *'the sole congenial soul in this godforsaken place.'*

BENNY HAVENS'S TAVERN, NR WEST PT. (DISMANTLED 1879)

It was against this background that New York's Washington Irving wrote two books, which are said to have made Americans more sympathetic to Christmas, and which also (significantly for the world) influenced Charles Dickens.

In his first book, *A Knickerbocker's History of New York*, 1809, an important character was a jolly, Dutch Saint Nicholas who travelled over the city on horseback and dropped presents through chimneys. Ten years later (in *The Sketch Book of Geoffrey Crayon, Gent.*, 1819), Irving recreated (in a 19th century English country-house setting) a romanticized version of England's abandoned, lavish 'Old Christmas.'

THE NEW YORK SANTA CLAUS OF 1844 (*NEW MIRROR* WEEKLY) - THE NIGHT IS NOT CHRISTMAS EVE, BUT 'THE NIGHT BEFORE NEW YEAR' [SEE CHAPTER 6]

ST NICHOLAS (R.W. WEIR, N.Y., 1838)

Irving and Dickens were admirers of one another's work; they corresponded with one another, and became friends. Dickens stayed at Irving's house, *Sunnyside [above]*, in Tarrytown,

SUNNYSIDE, N.Y.

THE TRIM SANTA CLAUS OF 1846 NEW YORK—COVER OF HARVEY B.
DODWORTH'S MUSIC SCORE (THE AMERICAN ANTIQUARIAN SOCIETY)

Part 1

*Makers &
Milestones
of Christmas*

New York, when he toured America in 1842 (the year before he wrote *A Christmas Carol*). If Irving had not reminded the English-speaking world (in his 1819 *Sketch Book*) of the way a fulsome celebration of Christmas could enrich lives, Dickens might never have written *A Christmas Carol*.

The effect of *A Christmas Carol* was so great that the author's name has become almost synonymous with Christmas, and

CHILDREN AT THE *STRIEZELMARKT* - OLDEST (1434) CHRISTMAS MARKET IN GERMANY (L. RICHTER 1803-84)

'AT THIS FESTIVE SEASON..., MR SCROOGE, ...WE SHOULD MAKE SOME SLIGHT PROVISION FOR THE POOR ...' (A. RACKHAM, 1915)

8

Keeping Christmas Well

A CHRISTMAS CAROL, DICKENS, ILLUSTRATED BY J. LEECH, 1843

with good reason. In a way that few other books have done, it changed lives for the better. It was an immediate popular and critical success when it came out on 19th December 1843. Before long, its publication came to have the status of an almost spiritual event. William Makepeace Thackeray said that *A Christmas Carol* was 'a national benefit, and to every man or woman who reads it, a personal kindness.' He described how the last two people he had heard speak of it had said of Dickens: 'God bless him.' Scottish writer, Margaret Oliphant, said that in the days of its first publication *A Christmas Carol* was seen as 'a new gospel,' and that the book was unique in that it made people behave better.

'CHRISTMAS CARNIVAL IN THE NEW YORK STOCK EXCHANGE' HARPER'S MONTHLY, 1885 (FROM NEW YORK PUBLIC LIBRARY)

11. **Robert Seymour** (1798–1836) was an English artist whose life and work crossed tragically with those of Dickens. Seymour published a series of pioneering Christmas illustrations in 1836. Some of these evoked the spirit of the idealised, traditional Christmas that was then being rediscovered in England; some were depictions of the baronial 'Old Christmas.' The illustrations were featured in *The Book of Christmas* by Thomas K. Hervey, published in 1836, seven years before *A Christmas Carol* appeared. The non-fiction book (its writing of lesser quality than its illustrations) was not a success.

A much respected artist and engraver in the 1830s, Seymour might be better known today if fate and publishers had not brought him together with Charles

Part 1

Makers & Milestones of Christmas

'ENJOYING CHRISTMAS' (R. SEYMOUR, *THE BOOK OF CHRISTMAS*, 1836)

ROBERT SEYMOUR SELFPORTRAIT C.1836 (MINIATURE, WATER-COLOUR ON IVORY)

'THE CHRISTMAS EVE MARKET' (R. SEYMOUR, *THE BOOK OF CHRISTMAS*, 1836)

Keeping Christmas Well

Dickens. Seymour is known to have originated the idea of *The Pickwick Papers*, and Dickens subsequently was approached to write its text.

Dickens wanted *The Pickwick Papers* to take a different direction than that suggested by Seymour's drawings. The writer and the artist had a meeting in 1836, fell out badly, and the next day the 38-year-old Seymour committed suicide. Seymour's widow openly blamed Dickens. As a result of the controversy, Seymour's reputation suffered, and he was largely forgotten. His wonderful, ground-breaking drawings for *The Book of Christmas* are used throughout this book.

'THE MISTLETOE BOUGH' (R.SEYMOUR, *THE BOOK OF CHRISTMAS*, 1836)

'BRINGING HOME CHRISTMAS'
(R. SEYMOUR, *THE BOOK OF CHRISTMAS*, 1836)

and Chronologically –

III. Pagan Rome and its Empire responsible, surprisingly, for many of the kindest and most decent aspirations of the Christmas season, and also for much of its gaiety and prettiness.

Rome's influential festivals of December and January are remembered for their jollity, but had surprisingly high ideals *[see chapter 1]*. Along with the games-playing, the feasting, and the decoration of the houses with greenery, there was a social expectation that the powerless would be treated equally with the powerful, the poor would be treated generously, and everyone would throw dignity to the winds. Without their residual influence, Christmas would be a much duller holiday.

Part 1

Makers & Milestones of Christmas

TEMPLE OF SATURN, ROME (PIRANESI, 18th CENT.)

THE FIRST PRINTED CHRISTMAS CARD, IN 1843, DESIGNED BY JOHN C. HORSLEY FOR HENRY COLE (FOUNDER OF THE VICTORIA & ALBERT MUSEUM, LONDON). 1,000 COPIES WERE PUBLISHED BY J. CUNDALL AT 1/- EACH. THE CARD SHOCKED SOME WITH ITS DEPICTION OF A CHILD DRINKING WINE. [*THIS IMAGE FROM BRIDWELL LIBRARY, S.M.U., DALLAS, ONE OF 10 REMAINING COPIES*]

IV. Saint Nicholas (c. 280–347).

ST NICHOLAS (*HARPER'S M.*, 1873)

Not much is known about Nicholas as provable fact (except that he was Bishop of Myra, in Turkey, and was at the formative church Council of Nicea in 325 AD) but he left behind nice legends. He is said to have been wealthy—and generous with his money. After his death, he was remembered not just for his gifts to the poor, but also for protecting the dignity of the recipient.

The most Christmas-relevant story about him concerns money he gave to an impoverished family (as dowries for three girls so that they could be married rather than sold into prostitution). Nicholas is said to have thrown the money into the family house through the window at night so that no one would know who had given it. (A variation of the story—one that would catch the popular imagination, and change history— is that he dropped part of the money

ST NICHOLAS DELIVERS DOWRIES (A. LORENZETTI, C. 1332)

down the chimney and it landed in the stocking of one of the daughters.) Not all of this was a tale for children, but from it developed the most child-friendly of all Christmas traditions—the mysterious arrival in the night of presents.

> …in many places, it was the custom for parents, on the vigil of St Nicholas (the evening of December 5th) to convey secretly presents of various kinds to their little sons and daughters who were taught to believe that they owed them to the kindness of St Nicholas

and his train, who, going up and down among the towns and villages, came in at the windows, though they were shut, and distributed them.
[—Rudolf Hospinian, Swiss writer, 1547-1626]

Nicholas became an object of veneration to surprisingly diverse groups—children, sailors, even pawnbrokers, and also, it seems, to virgins, because of his kindness to the three unmarried girls. This interesting account of his feast day in some convents was written in 1812:

Part 1

Makers & Milestones of Christmas

ST NICHOLAS VISITS A GIRLS' SCHOOL (SCHENKMAN, AMSTERDAM, C.1850)

In several convents it was customary, on the Eve of St Nicholas, for the Boarders to place each a silk stocking at the door of the apartment of the abbess, with a piece of paper enclosed, recommending themselves to Great St Nicholas of her chamber; and the next day they were called together to witness the Saint's attention, who never failed to fill the stockings with sweetmeats, and other trifles of that kind, with which these credulous virgins made a general feast. [from *Clavis Calendaria*, by John Brady, London, 1812]

The Protestant reformation had some effect on the customs of St Nicholas's day (the reformers did not approve of saints' feast days), but only in certain places and only superficially. In Protestant areas of Germany, for instance, the identity of the gift-giver was changed from St Nicholas to the Christ-Child (*Christkind*) and the date for present-giving was moved to Christmas. But

'CHRISTMAS DELIVERY' BY THE CHRIST-CHILD (JOSÉ FRAPPA 1854-1904)

Keeping Christmas Well

many other countries held on to the St Nicholas Day traditions, most significantly (for modern Christmas mythology) the Netherlands, where he goes under the names *Sint Nikolaas* or *Sinterklaas*, and where his feast day on 6th December (with its eve on the 5th) remains the occasion for children's presents, brought by him.

SINTERKLAAS IN WARTIME NETHERLANDS, DECEMBER 1944

St Nicholas first became significant in American life when Washington Irving published his fantasy *Knickerbocker's History of New York* on St Nicholas's Day, 6th December, 1809.

ST NICHOLAS, EUROPE (*I.L.N.* 1897)

Irving's jolly Nicholas had little in common with the austere European bishop; he smoked a 'mighty pipe,' travelled over rooftops on a horse, and took presents from his breeches' pockets, dropping them down chimneys. On St Nicholas's Day, he brought presents in a wagon. For children, the big difference with this St Nicholas was that he did not leave behind (or even wield!) a switch

DUTCH 'SINT NIKOLAAS' IN TRAVELLING CLOTHES (WITH A NAUGHTY BOY?) 1814

Part 1

Makers & Milestones of Christmas

'SINT NIKOLAAS—VERTELLINGEN VOOR DE JEUGD' ['SAINT NICHOLAS—STORIES FOR YOUNG PEOPLE'] BY REV. C. VAN SCHAICK, NETHERLANDS, 1852, DRAWN: C.W. MIELING, SCHIEDAM: ST NICHOLAS GREETED BY A REALLY NAUGHTY BOY...

'SINT NIKOLAAS - VERTELLINGEN VOOR DE JEUGD' ['SAINT NICHOLAS - STORIES FOR YOUNG PEOPLE'] BY REV. C. VAN SCHAICK, NETHERLANDS, 1852, DRAWN: C.W. MIELING, SCHIEDAM: ...RETRIBUTION.

Keeping Christmas Well

for the naughty, as he traditionally did in Europe, where the Saint's visit had always been a worrying lottery. Bad children did not face just an empty stocking or a lump of coal in it—but a punishment implement. In 19th century Netherlands, the Saint *[below]* might even take the naughty away in his bag.

ST NICHOLAS TAKES NAUGHTY CHILDREN IN HIS BAG (SCHENKMAN'S *ST NIKOLAAS EN ZIJN KNECHT* 1885 ED., *DRAWN:* J. VLIEGER, NETHERLANDS)

The birch rod, however, was not easy to get rid of anywhere, and it made a determined comeback in other American depictions of the children's gift-giver in the next decades. The first American *visual* depiction of Saint Nicholas (also titled '*SANCTE CLAUS*') *[< left]* was commissioned in 1810 (the year following Irving's 1809 book) by the New York Historical Society (of which Irving was a member). In this, the saint looks dour; and although the little girl is happy, the crying boy has been given nothing but a rod.

'SANCTE CLAUS' NEW YORK, 1810

It was traditional, it seems, for the unfortunate older boy to fare badly. In each of the Dutch works shown following—from the 17th and the 18th centuries—a boy (far left in each picture) is crying. The saint has left toys for the other children, but only a switch for the older boy.

Part 1
Makers & Milestones of Christmas

'THE FEAST OF SAINT NICHOLAS' (JAN STEEN, NETHERLANDS C. 1664)
—GIRL AT BACK LEFT HOLDS UP SHOE CONTAINING SWITCH

AMSTERDAM C. 1761—ONCE AGAIN, THE OLDER BOY *[AT LEFT]* IS CRYING, HAVING BEEN GIVEN ONLY A SWITCH IN HIS SHOE, WHILE HIS THREE YOUNGER SIBLINGS ENJOY TOYS AND CAKES. 'HET ST NICOLAAS FEEST' ['ST NICHOLAS'S DAY CELEBRATION'] (ENGRAVED BY J. HOUBRAKEN AFTER CORNELIS TROOST)

Keeping Christmas Well

AN UNUSUALLY HAPPY ENDING (BY 19th CENTURY ILLUSTRATION STANDARDS) TO A ST NICHOLAS VISIT. *ABOVE:* A BOY HIDES BEHIND HIS MOTHER AS THE SAINT ENTERS WITH A SWITCH. *BELOW:* THE SAINT LEAVES GIFTS FOR ALL THE CHILDREN—EVEN FOR THE OLDER BOY. [LUDWIG RICHTER, DRESDEN, 1852]

The image of the American St Nicholas/Santa Claus evolved rapidly in the second half of the 19th century and in the early 20th century. By 1910, he was well ahead of his time, as is clear from these illustrations in *St Nicholas Magazine*:

(*ST NICHOLAS MAGAZINE*, NEW YORK, 1910)

Part 1

Makers & Milestones of Christmas

(SAINT NICHOLAS MAGAZINE, NEW YORK, 1910)

SANTA: "MY, BUT THIS BEATS A SLEIGH AND REINDEER!"

and a Later Saint —

V. SAINT FRANCIS OF ASSISI (c.1181–1226).

To the early Church, Christmas was a time for addressing the serious business of man's redemption, not for celebrating. The faithful, however, had different ideas, and kept the holiday as if they were still pagans. The Church spent more than half a millennium condemning them for this. The much-loved and revolutionary Saint Francis, however, (at the start of the 13th century) took a more human view, focusing attention on the story of Bethlehem. Famously he re-created the Nativity scene with live animals. His influence gave legitimacy to the idea that Christmas should be a joyous celebration, centred on the birth of a baby.

ST FRANCIS & WOLF (BOUMARD FILS, PARIS, C.1900)

Keeping Christmas Well

< ST FRANCIS CREATES THE FIRST CRIB (IN 1223 AD, AT GRECCIO, ITALY), USING A LIVE OX AND ASS, (FRESCO BY GIOTTO DI BONDONE AT ASSISI BASILICA, C. 1300 AD)

ABOVE: 'ST FRANCIS PREACHING TO THE BIRDS' (FRESCO BY GIOTTO DI BONDONE, ASSISI, C. 1300)

RIGHT: 'CHRISTMAS TREE FOR THE BIRDS (HUNG WITH CHAINS OF NUTS AND SUET FOR THE WILD BIRDS)' *I.L.N.*, 1922 >

< 'A STABLE AT CHRISTMASTIME' (E.N. DOWNARD, *I.L.N.*, 1874)

'STABLE IN BETHLEHEM' (L. RICHTER, 1803-1884, DRESDEN) >

VI. Martin Luther (1483–1546).

By the late middle ages, the Catholic Church had given up trying to put a damper on the popular celebration of Christmas, a prolonged holiday which had grown steadily in exuberance throughout Europe.  (L. CRANACH ELDR, 1525) In the opinion of fun-lovers, these centuries were the holiday's heyday. The Protestant Reformation then brought a change. Some reformers disapproved of the idea of December 25th being celebrated at all as a religious holiday. As for the relentless frivolity, feasting, and decorations that were part of the season, these were abhorrent to them as exhibitions of paganism. The artistic Luther, however, maintained a true German love of Christmas: he wrote Christmas carols, is popularly credited with the idea of putting lights (candles) on a Christmas tree, and is certainly responsible for bringing the Christmas tree into churches.

Part 1

Makers & Milestones of Christmas

LUTHER & HIS FAMILY WITH CHRISTMAS TREE AT WITTENBERG C.1536 (C.A. SCHWERDGEBURTH, 1843)

A GERMAN CHRISTMAS TREE (L. RICHTER, 1864)

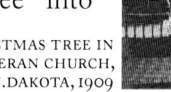

CHRISTMAS TREE IN LUTHERAN CHURCH, DWIGHT, N.DAKOTA, 1909

Keeping Christmas Well

and as for the Banning of Christmas—

A PURITAN STOPS THE GATHERING OF CHRISTMAS GREENERY (*THE GRAPHIC*, 1875)

VII. **MARCHMONT NEDHAM** (1620-1678)—an English writer/journalist of famously little principle, but memorable turn of phrase. Known for his willingness to support anyone in power, Nedham is in this list solely because of a few lines of verse he wrote about the twenty or so years (between 1640 and 1660) when Puritans, under the leadership of Oliver Cromwell, controlled the English Parliament. In terms of the sweep of history, this was not a long time, but Cromwell had an ability to make a big impression quickly. In Ireland, he is legendary as the perpetrator of the worst atrocities in the country's history. In England, one of his odder initiatives was the banning of Christmas.

Before Cromwell's ban, Christmas had been a robustly jolly holiday in England, and a very popular one. Traditionally, it was celebrated for weeks (or months), and involved the consumption of huge amounts of food and drink, playing games, gambling, dancing, wearing costumes and masks, decorating with holly and ivy, and often abandoning all the normal rules and hierarchies of life. Under the Puritans, every

CHRISTMAS DINNER BANNED (WILD TURKEY, *THE BIRDS OF AMERICA*, J. J. AUDUBON, 1827)

tradition of Christmas was banned: Church services were banned; mince pies were banned; plum pudding was banned; holly and ivy were banned; and in 1644, Christmas was ordered to be observed as a day of fasting—

HOLLY & IVY BANNED
(*DRAWING:* B. FOSTER, 1879)

Part 1

Makers & Milestones of Christmas

'to be kept with the more solemn humiliation, because it may call to remembrance our sins.'

The banning of Christmas *[see also chapter 9]* provoked fury and riots, and was written about at length by people of honour and principle—a group that did not include Nedham. (He was against the Puritans before they took power, supported them while they were in power, and against them again after they lost power. He was jailed at different times by each of the opposing sides, and each time he changed sides to secure his release.) No one, however, caught the absurd essence and effect of Cromwell's anti-Christmas laws as well as Nedham did in the following few lines:

CHRISTMAS SERVICES BANNED
(*DRAWING:* R.CALDECOTT, 1886)

> Gone are those golden days of yore
> When Christmas was a high day;
> Whose sports we now shall see no more,
> 'Tis turn'd into Good Friday.

(*OLD CHRISTMAS MASQUE,* 1850)

Keeping Christmas Well

VIII. EDMUND ANDROS (1637–1714), a little known and deeply unpopular colonial governor in New England. The reason this imperious and unsympathetic colonial administrator is on this list is that he happened to be the person (in 1681) who revoked the law banning the celebration of Christmas in Massachusetts. In 1659, the Puritan-dominated Massachusetts Bay Colony had made an order that anyone who stayed away from work or was found 'feasting' on Christmas Day was subject to a fine of five shillings for every offence. This was a popular law. The lifting of it (through intervention from London) was not. In 1686, an armed guard had to protect Andros when he went to church on Christmas Day.

ANDROS (ENGR. C.1890)

'MASON FAMILY CHILDREN DRESSED FOR CHURCH' (MASSACHUSETTS, 1670)

'RETURNING FROM CHURCH AT CHRISTMAS' (G. THOMAS, *I.L.N.*, 1855)

Part 1

Makers & Milestones of Christmas

IX. MAJOR HENRY LIVINGSTON JR. (1748–1828) *[< left]*, who almost certainly wrote the poem *A Visit from St Nicholas* (better known as *The Night Before Christmas*), which gave us our modern Santa and his reindeer; CLEMENT CLARKE MOORE (1779–1863) *[below]*, who was credited for more than a century-and-a-half with writing it; and DON FOSTER, Professor of English Literature and 'literary detective.'

A VISIT FROM ST NICHOLAS
[PRANG & CO. EDITION BOSTON, 1864]

A Visit from St Nicholas was first published in the Troy *Sentinel*, New York State, in 1823 (anonymously, as was usual at the time). It caught the public's fancy, and was frequently re-published. The first time an author's name was attached to it was in 1837—nine years after Livingston's death—when it was attributed to Clement Clarke Moore, a wealthy New York Bible scholar, and son of an Episcopal bishop. The poem gave Moore his greatest success. He officially claimed it as his own in 1844, when he published a volume of forty-four poems which included it.

WHEN OUT ON THE LAWN THERE AROSE SUCH A CLATTER, I SPRANG FROM THE BED TO SEE WHAT WAS THE MATTER.

[DRAWING: 1896 M^CLOUGHLIN BROS. ED.]

Keeping Christmas Well

Major Henry Livingston Jr., a War of Independence veteran, was a farmer and surveyor, of Dutch-Scottish background, who lived at Poughkeepsie, New York State. He wrote (and sometimes

'THE SEAT OF HENRY LIVINGSTON ESQ (SNR.) AT POUGHKEEPSIE' (DRAWN BY H. LIVINGSTON JR, 1791)

published, but always anonymously) a good deal of light verse. The Livingston family says *A Visit from St Nicholas* was written around 1805 and, in 1822, was brought innocently from Livingston's house by a visitor (a governess in the Moore household) who liked the poem and asked for a copy of it. In 1823 (apparently without the knowledge of Moore) the poem was sent to the Troy *Sentinel* for publication. Third parties

'NOW! DASHER,
NOW! DANCER,
NOW! PRANCER,
AND VIXEN,
'ON! COMET, ON!
CUPID, ON!
DUNDER AND
BLIXEM; ...'*

*ORIGINAL NAMES
(& PUNCTUATION)

(DRAWING: M^cLOUGHLIN BROS. ED., 1896)

assumed the anonymous poem had been written by Moore, and later his name was put to it. Livingston's family did not learn until about 1860 that Moore had claimed authorship.

Fortunately for Livingston's claim, each of the men left behind a body of verse, which in style could hardly be more different. On reading both men's works, any neutral with an ear—even with a tenth of an ear—is going to conclude that Livingston wrote *A Visit from St Nicholas*. It's not just a question of rhythm and vocabulary—it's also the soul. Livingston's verses really do not sound like anyone else's: they are an unusual combination of wit, perkiness, and cosiness. If Santa Claus were to write verse, you would expect him to write like Livingston.

The similarities of metre and vocabulary between *A Visit from St Nicholas* and Livingston's other work also catch the ear— the rhyming of 'clatter' and 'matter,' for instance, and of 'elf' and 'self':

(*A VISIT...*, PRANG ED., BOSTON, 1864)

> When out on the lawn there arose such a clatter,
> I sprang from the bed to see what was the matter.
> [—from *A Visit from St Nicholas*].
>   And now the end of all this clatter
>   Is but a small and trifling matter;
> [—from Livingston's *A New Year's Address*, 1787].
> Well, Madam, the long and the short of the clatter,
> For mumbling & mincing will not better the matter,
> [—from Livingston's *A Tenant of Mrs van Kleek*, 1787].

The narrator of this *Mistress van Kleek* poem is a tenant who had promised three hogs (three sows, in fact) to his landlady, and he goes on to express these classic lines:

> The sows, my sweet madam,
>   the sows I repeat
> Which you and your
>   household expected
>   to eat,
> Instead of attending their corn and their swill
> Gave way to an ugly he-sow's wicked will.

SO UP TO THE HOUSE-TOP THE COURSERS THEY FLEW, WITH THE SLEIGH FULL OF TOYS —AND ST. NICHOLAS TOO: (DRAWING: 1864, PRANG ED.)

As for 'elf' and 'self':

> He was chubby and plump, a right jolly old elf,
> And I laugh'd when I saw him, in spite of myself;
> [—from *A Visit from St Nicholas*].

Keeping Christmas Well

Take the name of the swain, a forlorn witless elf
Who was changed to a flower for admiring himself,
[—from Livingston's pre-1789 *The Dance*].

Livingston's poems were genuinely funny. The following, for instance, was his male take on the hairdressing and hooped skirts of the women of his time:

(COIFFURE, 1780s)

AND THEN IN A TWINKLING, I HEARD ON THE ROOF THE PRANCING AND PAWING OF EACH LITTLE HOOF.
(M^cLOUGHLIN BROS. ED. 1896, N.Y.)

> For us (and I blush while
>   I speak, I declare)
> The charming enchanters
>   be-torture their hair,
> Till gently it rises,
>   and swells like a knoll,
> Thirty inches at least
>   from the dear little poll. ...
> Then hoops at right angles that
>   hang from the knees
> And hoops at the hips, in
>   connection with these,
> Set the fellows presumptuous,
>   who court an alliance,
> And ev'ry pretender, at awful
>   defiance.
> [—Livingston, *The Poughkeepsie Advertiser*, 1787]

(GALERIE DES MODES, 1780s)

Moore's style, on the other hand, seems to come from a different world. Whatever else Moore was, he was not funny. He wrote in 'a moralizing vein' as one critic, Winthrop P. Tyron, put it [*Christian Science Monitor*, 4th August 1920]. In one poem from his 1844 collection (*The Pig and the Rooster*) Moore made an attempt at humour, but with an almost embarrassing lack of success '—so sadly are wit, fancy, and imagination

HE WAS DRESS'D ALL IN FUR, FROM HIS
   HEAD TO HIS FOOT,
AND HIS CLOTHES WERE ALL
   TARNISH'D WITH ASHES AND SOOT;
[DRAWING: *PRANG & CO.*, BOSTON, 1864]

Part 1

*Makers &
Milestones
of Christmas*

dismembered and cast into the tub,' was how Tyron summed it up.

The following passage is cited by one modern reviewer (*Barnesandnoble.com*) as being 'typical' of Moore:

> To me 'tis giv'n your virtue to secure
>   From custom's force and pleasure's dangerous lure.
> For if, regardless of my friendly voice,
>   In Fashion's gaudy scenes your heart rejoice,
> Dire punishments shall fall upon your head:
>   Disgust, and fretfulness and secret dread. …
>   [—Clement Clarke Moore]

In spite of all of this, however, and frustratingly for the Livingstons, *A Visit from St Nicholas* had been associated with the name Clement C. Moore for a long time. In fact, Moore was known for nothing else, and was loved for the poem, which had become a foundation stone of Christmas for many. If that foundation stone were to be taken away and replaced, the family needed a heavy lifter. That was where Don Foster came in. A professor of English literature at Vassar College, he had solved the mystery of who had written the best-seller *Primary Colours* (which featured a fictional character

A VISIT FROM ST. NICHOLAS
THE STUMP OF A PIPE HE HELD
   TIGHT IN HIS TEETH,
AND THE SMOKE IT ENCIRCLED HIS
   HEAD LIKE A WREATH.
(*THE POETS OF AMERICA*, N.Y., 1840)

HE SPOKE NOT A WORD, BUT WENT STRAIGHT TO HIS WORK, AND FILL'D ALL THE STOCKINGS; THEN TURN'D WITH A JERK, (DRAWING: T.C. BOYD, N.Y., 1848)

clearly based on Bill Clinton) by analysis of writing styles; and he did writing analysis for the FBI, including in the case of the 'Unabomber' suspect Ted Kaczynski.

Livingston's direct descendant, Mary Van Deusen, approched Don Foster; and after investigation, Foster concluded that Livingston, and not Clement Moore, was the author of the poem. [His account of how and why he reached this conclusion makes fascinating reading in his book *Author Unknown*, New York, 2000.]

So what would Livingston himself have thought of all this? One of his verses, *Careless Philosopher's Soliloquy*, suggests that he would not have been bothered too much one way or the other:

> I rise when I please,
>   when I please I
>   lie down,
> Nor seek, what I
>   care not a rush
>   for, renown;
> The rattle called
>   wealth I have
>   learnt to despise,
> Nor aim to be either
>   important
>   or wise.

AND LAYING HIS FINGER ASIDE OF HIS NOSE
AND GIVING A NOD, UP THE CHIMNEY HE ROSE. (DRAWING: DARLEY 1862)

BUT I HEARD HIM EXCLAIM,
   ERE HE DROVE OUT OF SIGHT—
HAPPY CHRISTMAS TO ALL,
   AND TO ALL A GOOD NIGHT.
      (DRAWING: THOS. NAST, 1869)

[FOR FULL TEXT, AS FIRST PUBLISHED (TROY *SENTINEL*, 1823), SEE CHAPTER 14]

X. *The Children's Friend*, 1821.

One intriguing suggestion Foster made about Clement Clarke Moore's writing did not relate to *A Visit from Saint Nicholas* at all, but to another poem published anonymously as an eight-page illustrated booklet in New York in 1821: the interesting, but alarming, *The Children's Friend*. Foster suggests that Moore wrote this poem—which was some poem. Not surprisingly, it is little known. Only two copies of the 1821 booklet are said to exist, one of which is in the possession of the American Antiquarian Society (from which these images were taken). It is thought that an innocent mix-up by a third party between the two poems might have led to the misapprehension—which then took root—that Moore had written *The Night Before Christmas*.

The steady friend of virtuous youth,
The friend of duty, and of truth,
Each Christmas eve he joys to come
Where love and peace have made their home

The Children's Friend forms an interesting link in the evolution of Santa, because he has just about been given his modern name (Santeclaus) and it includes a visual depiction of a reindeer and sleigh on a rooftop. As Saint Nicholas did in *The*

Old Santeclaus with much delight
His reindeer drives this frosty night,
O'er chimney tops, and tracks of snow,
To bring his yearly gifts to you.

Night Before Christmas, Santeclaus makes his deliveries on Christmas Eve (rather than on Saint Nicholas's Eve, the fifth of December).

In other respects, however, the gift-giver moves back in time and back to Europe, because he carries a worrying *'long, black birchen rod.'*

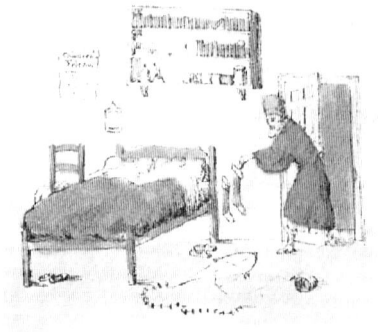

Through many houses he has been,
And various beds and stockings seen;
Some, white as snow, and neatly mended,
Others, that seem'd for pigs intended.

This Santa is anything but jolly. He inspects bedrooms (finding some of them *'seem'd for pigs intended'*); his switch (tied with a bow) is the most clearly drawn image in the book, and the gifts he brings are not much fun:

> No drums to stun their Mother's ear,
>> Nor swords to make their sisters fear;
> But pretty books to store their mind
>> With knowledge of each various kind.

He sleigh is even fitted with a bookshelf. The lines that might leave a child with nightmares come at the end, and are introduced with a tiny hanged man!

> But where I found the children naughty,
>> In manners rude, in temper haughty,
> Thankless to parents, liars, swearers,
>> Boxers, or cheats, or base tale-bearers,
> I left a long, black birchen rod,
>> Such as the dread command of God
> Directs a Parent's hand to use
>> When virtue's path his sons refuse.

Part 1

Makers & Milestones of Christmas

CHRISTMAS TREE, AT WANDSBEKER PALACE, GERMANY, IN 1796 (MID-19th CENTURY WOODCUT BY HUGO BÜRKNER, SHOWING A GOLDEN APPLE BEING PLUCKED FROM THE CANDLE-LIT TREE ON CHRISTMAS EVE)

XI. PRINCE ALBERT OF SAXE-COBURG & GOTHA, and MR MIKE CARR, logger, New York.

The German Prince Albert had grown up experiencing the enviable, sumptuous German Christmas, centred on the Christmas tree. He wanted his own children to know the same pleasure. It seems he was successful in this: '... their delight in the Christmas trees is not less than ours used to be,' he reported.

In December 1848, a print of Queen Victoria, Prince Albert, and their children surrounding a decorated Christmas tree was published in the *Illustrated London News [right>]*. The effect of this staid print was surprising. Before its publication, the popularity

ORIGINAL 1848 ILLUSTRATION (*I.L.N.*)

Keeping Christmas Well

< C.1816 ILLUSTRATION OF THE 1803 GERMAN CHRISTMAS-TREE POEM BY J. P. HEBEL, *'DIE MUTTER AM CHRIST-ABEND'* [–'THE MOTHER ON CHRISTMAS EVE'].

[AN 1826 ILLUSTRATION OF THE SAME POEM IS SHOWN BELOW LEFT]

of the Christmas tree had been confined to German-speaking countries, and to royal courts of Europe. ...*In many parts of Germany...a large bough is set up in the principal room at Christmas time, the smaller branches of which are hung with little presents suitable to the different members of the household...* wrote William Sandys in London in 1833, confirming the English unfamiliarity then with the Christmas tree. The 1848 print, however, caught the public imagination in a major way. Well-to-do households were the first to incorporate the Christmas tree into their domestic decoration, and eventually its popularity would spread to all levels of society.

CHRISTABEND (B. ZIX, GERMANY, 1826)

AMERICAN ADAPTATION (WITHOUT CROWN, SASH, MOUSTACHE, ETC) 1850, *GODEY'S LADY'S BOOK*, PHILADELPHIA

Two years later, in December 1850, an altered version of the print was published in the U.S. in *Godey's Lady's Book*. In order to make the figures look American, Victoria's crown had been taken away, along with Albert's moustache and sash. In America, also, the effect of this print was culture-changing, even though it was neither the first nor the most appealing image of a Christmas tree drawn or published in the U.S.

The first *published* Christmas-tree drawing was the charming frontispiece of an 1836 collection of essays by Hermann Bokum, *The Stranger's Gift [>]*.

FRONTISPIECE TO *THE STRANGER'S GIFT*, BOSTON, 1836

THE FIRST KNOWN U.S. DRAWING OF A CHRISTMAS TREE (J.L. KRIMMEL, 1810S)

The first known U.S. drawing of a Christmas tree *[above]* was done from life around 1815 by a German immigrant to Pennsylvania, John Lewis (Johann Ludwig) Krimmel (1786-1821).

Still, it was the 1850 drawing in *Godey's Lady's Book* that made the breakthrough. The illustration received huge attention, and can be credited with launching not only a much-loved American Christmas tradition, but also an industry.

A year later, in 1851, New York had its first Christmas tree lot when a logger, Mike Carr, rented an area of city sidewalk for $1, and sold cut trees from it. It is assumed he did a roaring business, because in 1852, the rent for that sidewalk had gone up to $100.

CHRISTMAS TREE MARKET AT BARCLAY STREET FREIGHT STATION, NEW YORK CITY, C.1900 [U.S. LIBRARY OF CONGRESS]

ABOVE: ONE OF THE OLDEST REPRESENTATIONS OF A CANDLE-LIT TREE ON CHRISTMAS EVE, DRAWN IN ZURICH BY J. M. USTERI C. 1775 (& ENGRAVED BY J. H. LIPS IN 1799), SHOWING ST NIKOLAUS— 'WHO BRINGS A GIFT-LADEN TREE TO ALL GOOD SWISS CHILDREN.'

'CHRISTMAS TREE WITH CHILDREN'S GIFTS'(L. RICHTER, GERMANY, C. 1847)

XII. THOMAS NAST, cartoonist, 1840–1902.

ABOVE: THE NORTH POLE CHRISTMAS TREE, BY THOMAS NAST (FROM *SANTA CLAUS AND HIS WORKS*, NEW YORK, 1869)

SANTA'S MAIL.—'FROM NAUGHTY CHILDREN'S PARENTS' (*TALL PILE*), & 'FROM GOOD CHILDREN'S PARENTS' (*SMALL PILE*) [T. NAST, *HARPER'S WEEKLY*, 1871]

Part 1

Makers & Milestones of Christmas

The German-born political cartoonist THOMAS NAST ultimately gave almost-final form to the appearance of the modern Santa Claus. His first drawing of Santa, however, [>] which appeared on the cover of  Harper's Weekly in January 1863 during the American Civil War, was different—because he dressed Santa (who was bringing presents to Union soldiers) more or less in the Union flag. This is said to have been an effective piece of wartime propaganda—an unwelcome message to the Confederate Army that Santa was on the side of the Union. In another Harper's Civil War illustration from 1863 by Nast [below], a Union soldier, home on Christmas furlough, is reunited with his family, and Santa [at left] (now in his civilian clothes) delivers presents for the children. (T. NAST, H.W., 1863)

Nast did a large number of Santa drawings for Harper's Weekly over more than two decades, and his drawings also were published in books, including, in 1869, in an enchanting children's picture and verse book *Santa Claus and His Works*. The text was written by George P. Webster, and is memorable for giving Santa an official residence [>] at the North Pole:

SANTA AT HOME (*SANTA CLAUS AND HIS WORKS*, 1869)

Part 1

Makers & Milestones of Christmas

> His home through the long summer months, you must know,
> Is near the North Pole, in the ice and the snow.

XIII. **U.S. PRESIDENT ULYSSES S. GRANT**, under whose presidency, Christmas Day was finally made a Federal holiday in the U.S. in 1870.

XIV. **VALENTINE DAVIES** (1905–1961), writer of the 1947 film *Miracle on 34th Street*. It is said that he started his screenplay in 1944 while in the U.S. Coast Guard, inspired by his dislike of the commercialization of Christmas. His plot did not fight the reality of shops and shopping as an integral part of Christmas, but sold the idea that if a shop became a force for good, it would do better business. An engaging Christmas script *[see chapter 7]*.

XV. **COL. HARRY SHOUP**, United States Air Force. Every Christmas, the U.S. Air Force tracks Santa on part of his journey around

the world. The tradition started in 1955 when a newspaper advertisement invited children to phone Santa Claus on Christmas Eve *[>]*, but accidentally printed the wrong number. A child phoned the number given, and instead of getting through to Santa, reached Colonel Harry Shoup, the senior officer on duty at the then Continental Air Defence Command Operations Center in Colorado Springs Colorado—on the hotline that would be expected to ring only if the Russians were attacking. Col. Shoup rose brilliantly to the occasion, giving instructions that Santa Claus be tracked and his location given to all the children who phoned that night.

TRACKING SANTA, 19th CENT., WITH MAP (T. NAST, 1885)

XVI. THE YEAR 1958— when Christmas was declared a public holiday in Scotland. Before then, it had been an ordinary working day and school day. The Scots famously celebrated New Year; but, at an official level, Christmas was ignored (the result, it is said, of the strong influence of the Calvinism John Knox had introduced to Scotland in the 16th century). Several decades later, Scotland declared the 26th December to be a public holiday as well.

NEW YEAR'S EVE AT TRON CHURCH, (*CASSELL'S OLD & NEW EDINBURGH*, 1882)

and Finally –

XVII. **The unknown author** of a 17th century *Christmas Eve Hymn* from the west of Ireland (*Dán d'Oidhche Nodlag*) with English translation (a brilliant one) by Douglas Hyde.

For all those whose Christmas centres around the Nativity, the degree to which these lines from that hymn evoke a sense of the unfathomable is unsurpassed:

> ...Little babe who art so great,
>   Child so young who art so old,
> In the manger small his room,
>   Whom not heaven itself could hold.
> ...Father—not more old than thou?
>   Mother—younger can it be?
> Older, younger is the son,
>   Younger, older she than he.

MADONNA & BABY (MARIANNE PREINDELSBERGER STOKES, C. 1907)

(T.NAST, *HARPER'S WEEKLY*, 1886)

A Note re Part II

The history of Christmas in this book comes from documents. *Theories* about pre-documented, ancient origins of Christmas customs (such as possible practices of the Celts and ancient Northern European tribes to mark the winter solstice of late December) are not much considered, because there is no certainty about them: opinions differ and evolve over time.

'The farther off we live from any given time or history, the more we know about it,' wrote the venerable antiquarian, W. Sandys, in 1852. This book does not subscribe to that thinking. We know, from documents, the extent to which Rome—first pagan Rome, and then Christian Rome—shaped our modern Christmas, because Greek and Roman authors left us accounts, and this book goes back no earlier than their written record.

PART II

CHAPTER 1

The Merry

Where it Came From and How it Survived

'The Best of Days'
—Catullus

Keeping Christmas Well

1. You say that pagan Rome had a big influence on our Christmas customs, but in what way?

—Nearly all of our most appealing Christmas customs come from two great Roman festivals: the Saturnalia of 17th to 23rd December and the Kalends at the beginning of January.

2. What do you mean?

—Well, have a look at the following set of 'rules.' Although they seem like rules for celebrating a particularly benevolent and generous Christmas, in fact they predated Christmas. They were conventions for celebrating the Saturnalia, set down (for fun) in the second century AD by Lucian, a Greek rhetorician.—

'A MERRY CHRISTMAS AND A HAPPY NEW YEAR' (K. MEADOWS, *CHRISTMAS POEMS & PICTURES*, 1864)

'BRINGING IN CHRISTMAS' (HARVEY, *CHRISTMAS POEMS & PICTURES*, 1864)

GENERAL RULES

All business, be it public or private,
is forbidden during the feast
days, save such as tends to
sports and solace and delight.
Let none follow their avocations
saving cooks and bakers.

BAKER'S, POMPEII, 79 AD

Chapter 1

The Merry
Christmas
—Where it
Came From

'FETCHING HOME THE CHRISTMAS DINNER FROM THE BAKER'S' (J. LEECH, LONDON, 1848)

All men shall be equal, slave and free, rich and
poor, with one another.
Anger, resentment, threats are contrary to law.
No discourse shall be either composed or delivered,
except it be witty and lusty, conducing to
mirth and jollity.

MERRY CHRISTMAS TO YOU (R. SEYMOUR, *THE BOOK OF CHRISTMAS*, 1836)

CHRISTMAS DINNER (R. SEYMOUR, *THE BOOK OF CHRISTMAS*, 1836)

RULES FOR THE TABLE

Every man shall take place as chance may direct;
Dignities and birth and wealth shall give no precedence;
All shall be served with the same wine...
Every man's portion of meat shall be alike.
When the rich man shall feast his slaves, let his friends serve with him.

C.79 AD, WOMAN SERVES A TRAVELLER, POMPEII WALL-PAINTING

ALL TRAVELLERS AS THEY DO PASS ON THEIR WAY AT GENTLEMEN'S HALLS ARE INVITED TO STAY, ...
NAY THE POOR SHALL NOT WANT, BUT HAVE FOR RELIEF PLUM-PUDDING, GOOSE, CAPON, MINC'D PIES AND ROAST BEEF
...
(—ENGLISH CAROL, *EVANS' OLD BALLADS*, 1784)

RIGHT: TRAVELLERS SEEK CHRISTMAS HOSPITALITY AT A MEDIEVAL ENGLISH MANOR > (ENGR.: H. VIZETELLY, *CHRISTMAS WITH THE POETS*, 1851)

3. Was present-giving a part of the Saturnalia?

—Yes, and at their most idealistic, the Saturnalia present-giving conventions seem to have been very nice ones. The rich were to give to the poor presents of money, clothing, or vessels. The poor were to give presents in return, but according to their needs and, interestingly, according to their talents.—

RULES FOR GIFTS

A poor man of learning should give an ancient book, but of good omen and festive humour, or a writing of his own after his ability. For the unlearned, let him send a garland or grains of frankincense.

Chapter 1

The Merry Christmas —Where it Came From

MAKING GIFTS (T. NAST, *SANTA CLAUS AND HIS WORKS*, NEW YORK, 1869)

4. But Lucian wasn't writing as a historian?

—No, but in the same way that popular Christmas songs and movies reflect the ideals of the modern Christmas, Lucian distilled the ideals of the Saturnalia.

5. What was the Saturnalia anyway?

—It was a festival that honoured Saturn, the Roman god of the seed-sowing.

6. Why would there be a big festival to honour a god of seed-sowing?

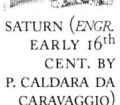

SATURN (*ENGR.* EARLY 16th CENT. BY P. CALDARA DA CARAVAGGIO)

—Saturn was also the mythical king of a Utopian Golden Age, when everyone was happy, innocent, equal, and at peace. The Saturnalia was a recreation of that Utopia.

(T. NAST, *HARPER'S WEEKLY*, 1873)

7. So the Saturnalia wasn't a great debauch?

—Not really. It just suffers from an evocative name. It was a festival, of course: schools were closed, slaves had unusual licence, there were banquets, wine flowed, and Rome was Rome. It was not a great week for stuffed-shirts or for the hierarchical, but it had an admirable purpose.

'CHRISTMAS IN THE COUNTRY,' S. COLLINGS, ENGLAND, 1791

8. But it sounds …

—Yes, it *sounds* like (and gets confused with) the *Bacchanalia* celebrations (which honoured Bacchus, god of wine, and which had been suppressed in 186 BC because of their excesses) but was a very different festival.

'NOËL EN FAMILLE' (RUDAUX, FRANCE, C.1886)

9. I see.

—In fact it was a festival of idealism. The Saturnalia brought fun into houses (the serious

Pliny the Younger kept to his room during it 'when the rest of the house is noisy with the licence of the holiday and festive cries'). Publius Papinius Statius wrote: *Never shall age destroy so holy a day! For how many years shall this festival abide!* Interestingly, even the severe early Christian church, which relentlessly condemned pagan festivals, never much criticized the Saturnalia.

49

Chapter 1

The Merry Christmas —Where it Came From

'CHRISTMAS MORNING' (C.LARSSON, SWEDEN, 1894)

10. The church really did not criticize the Saturnalia?

—No it did not. But there was a not-dissimilar Roman new-year festival, which the church never stopped criticizing. It had a more prosaic name, however, and has been largely forgotten—the *Kalends* of January.

11. Was that the same as our New Year?

—In fact it was like New Year, Christmas,

'CHRISTMAS ON A BATTLESHIP' (*THE GRAPHIC*, 1900)

Halloween, and more. This Roman Kalends (or *Calends*) festival started on January 1st, about a week after the Saturnalia ended. It lasted officially for three days but tended to continue for five days.

12. What kind of festival was the Kalends?

—It involved giving gifts (*strenae*), feasting, wearing costumes and masks, gambling, and a universal disregard for hierarchy (between rich and poor, master and slave, man and woman). We have been left a vivid account of the Kalends by a Greek writer, Libanius, who lived in the fourth century—

PLAYING CARDS, 'CHRISTMAS EVE' (J. BURNET, 1815)

> The festival of the Kalends is celebrated everywhere as far as the limits of the Roman Empire extend. …Everywhere may be seen carousals and well-laden tables; luxurious abundance is found in the houses of the rich, but also in the houses of the poor, better food than usual is put upon the table. The impulse to spend seizes everyone. He who through the whole year has taken pleasure in saving and piling up his pence, becomes suddenly extravagant. He who erstwhile was accustomed

'NEW YEAR'S EVE' (G. CRUIKSHANK, *ALMANAC*, 1838)

Chapter 1

The Merry Christmas —Where it Came From

and preferred to live poorly, now at this feast enjoys himself as much as his means will allow ... People are not only generous towards themselves, but also towards their fellow-men. A stream of presents pours itself out on all sides. ... The highroads and footpaths are covered with whole processions of laden men and beasts.

ABOVE: A PROCESSION (CARTHAGE, MOSAIC C. 2nd CENTURY AD, *LOUVRE MUSEUM*)

BELOW: MR BROWN MAKES HIS WAY HOME THROUGH A LONDON FOG, LEADING HIS BEARERS OF HOLLY, A WASSAIL BOWL, A YULE LOG, AND A BOAR'S HEAD (E. & G. DALZIEL, *CHRISTMAS COMES BUT ONCE A YEAR*, 1850)

... As the thousand flowers which burst forth everywhere are the adornment of Spring, so are the thousand presents poured out on all sides, the decoration of the Kalends feast. It may be justly said that it is the fairest time of the year. ... The Kalends festival banishes all that is connected with toil, and allows men to give themselves up

CHRISTMAS PRESENTS.

'CHRISTMAS PRESENTS' (R.SEYMOUR, *THE BOOK OF CHRISTMAS*, 1836)

Keeping Christmas Well

to undisturbed enjoyment. From the minds of young people, it removes two kinds of dread: the dread of the schoolmaster and the dread of the stern pedagogue. The slave also it allows, so far as possible, to breathe the air of freedom. ... Another great quality of the festival is that it teaches men not to hold too fast to their money, but to part with it and let it pass into other hands.

[—Libanius, fourth century AD]

ABOVE: 'CHRISTMAS SHOPPING, LONDON' (I.L.N., 1850)

'CHRISTMAS MARKET, NUREMBERG' (L. RICHTER, 1840)

Chapter 1

The Merry Christmas —Where it Came From

ABOVE: 'CHRISTMAS MARKET' IN STOCKHOLM (OTTO MANKELL, 1874) [*JULMARKNAD PÅ STORTORGET, 1874*]

ABOVE: 'THE CHRISTMAS TREE MARKET IN BERLIN' (*ILLUSTRATED LONDON NEWS*, 1905)

'WASHINGTON MARKET,' LOWER WEST SIDE (NOW TRIBECA), NEW YORK (*HARPER'S WEEKLY*, N.Y., CHRISTMAS 1874)

13. Was that it ?

—No, there was more. The cheerful Kalends also gave rise to many surviving New Year's (as well as Christmas) customs, and these may have been what really drew the ire

'CHRISTMAS MARKET, VIENNA' (W. GAUSE, 1894)

of the church. This is a paraphrase of Libanius's description of the Eve of Kalends (i.e. New Year's Eve). *[The emphasis is the author's]*—

Few people go to bed; most go about the streets with singing and leaping and all sorts of mockery. *The severest moralist utters no blame on this occasion.* When morning begins to dawn they decorate their houses with laurels and other greenery, and at daybreak may go to bed to sleep off their intoxication, for many deem it necessary at this

ABOVE: 'THE SEVEREST MORALIST UTTERS NO BLAME' (E.&G. DALZIEL, *CHRISTMAS COMES BUT ONCE A YEAR*, 1850)

GATHERING HOLLY (*I.L.N.*, 1883)

'SEEING-IN THE NEW YEAR' (R. SEYMOUR, *THE BOOK OF CHRISTMAS*, 1836)

feast to follow the flowing bowl. On the 1st of January money is distributed to the populace; on the 2nd no more presents are given: it is customary to stay at home playing dice, masters and slaves together. On the 3rd there is racing; on the 4th the festivities begin to decline, but they are not altogether over on the 5th. [Libanius, 4th century AD, also C.A. Miles, 1912.]

DICE-PLAYERS, FRESCO POMPEII, C. 79 AD

14. Nice. Did he mention any other customs?

—Well, Libanius didn't mention every custom. Some customs we know of largely from church condemnations of them: the wearing of costumes and masks, for instance, including the wearing of women's clothes by men (and vice versa) and the dressing up in the hides of animals. It would seem that the New Year's Eve masquerade party—think of the wild party on the train in the film *Trading Places*, and the plot-turning gorilla costume *[above]*—has come through time almost unchanged from the Kalends pattern.

MASKS, HERCULANEUM FRESCO, C. 79 AD

MASK, SEVILLE, MOSAIC, C. 250 AD

Chapter 1

The Merry Christmas
—*Where it Came From*

TRADING PLACES, 1983

15. But was Libanius really reliable, or was he maybe a bit dissolute himself?

No, Libanius (314-393 AD) was not dissolute. He taught St Basil and St Chrysostom. Yet Libanius clearly thought the Kalends was just a very good festival, and on the basis of his account, it is hard to disagree with him. If Dickens and Hollywood put their heads together, they could hardly have come up with a more good-hearted Christmas festival than Libanius described.

(BY J.T.LUCAS, *I.L.N.*, 1876)

16. But the church didn't go for the Kalends?

—No. In a big way, it disliked the Kalends; and

its dislike of the festival developed into one of history's longest religious

(R. CALDECOTT, 1886)

wars, but the only one that was harmless (and funny). On the one side was the power of the pre-Reformation Christian Church and on the other was the fun introduced into Christmas celebrations by the pagan Kalends.

'NEW YEAR'S EVE IN IRELAND' (*HARPER'S WEEKLY*, 1870)

17. Who won?

—Fun won.

18. How long did the war last?

—From the 4th century to the 11th century, the Church relentlessly tried to end the Kalends customs, even demanding for a time (in France) that people fast during the first three days of New Year ('fast with litanies,' in fact) instead of feasting and partying in the streets. There was little enthusiasm for this.

'CHRISTMAS IN A TAVERN,' 1775

In *The Medieval Stage* (Oxford, 1903), E.K. Chambers sums up the church's determined, but hopeless, struggle as follows:

> Homily followed homily, canon followed canon, capitulary followed capitulary, penitential

followed penetential, for half a thousand years. But the Kalends died hard. When Boniface was tackling them amongst the Franks in the middle of the eighth century, he was sorely hampered by the bad example of their continued prevalence at the very gates of the Vatican; and when Burchardus was making his collection of heathen observances in the eleventh century, those of the Kalends were still to be included. Chambers lists forty excerpts from such denunciations, ranging in date from the fourth century to the eleventh, and coming from Spain, Italy, Antioch, northern Africa, Constantinople, Germany, England, and France.

Chapter 1

The Merry Christmas —Where it Came From

MASKERS SURROUND A PRIEST IN ROME (ENGR. 1872)

19. But it finally gave up?

—Yes. At least, the pre-Reformation Catholic church gave up in the 11th century.

20. And then?

'CHRISTMAS FOR EVER!'(J.GILBERT, 1864)

—Then the next few centuries were said to be the best ones ever for Christmas in Europe. The Christmas holiday was prolonged, public, and communal.

21. And after that?

—Then the Protestant Reformation had an effect. Christmas's worst moments came in the 16th and

17th centuries, when the Calvinists and Puritans were able to ban the holiday for a time in some places.

22. Still, Christmas survived.

—Yes, Christmas (with all its pagan baggage, for good or bad) is still with us.

LIFE IN LONDON— TOM AND JERRY (1821)

'The one feast in the year in which paganism made its most startling and persistent recoil upon Christianity,' was Chambers's neat summary of the long Christmas war.

A CHRISTMAS MUMMING PLAY (*DRAWN:* G. BROWNE, 1886)

'CHRISTMAS ON A MAN-OF-WAR' (H. ROTH, *HARPER'S WEEKLY*, 1902)

MID-20th-CENTURY OFFICE CHRISTMAS PARTY IN *THE APARTMENT*, 1960

Chapter 1

*The Merry
Christmas
—Where it
Came From*

'COWBOYS COMING TO TOWN FOR CHRISTMAS' (F. REMINGTON, *HARPER'S WEEKLY*, 1889)

'CHRISTMAS ON AN ICEFLOE' (AUSTRO-HUNGARIAN POLAR EXPEDITION OF 1872-74, *ILLUSTRATED LONDON NEWS*, 1874)

F.O.C. DARLEY (*A VISIT FROM SAINT NICHOLAS*, PUBL. JAMES G. GREGORY, NEW YORK, 1862)

CHAPTER 2
The Traditional but Surprising Christmas Calendar:

The Forty Days of Christmas

1. Why do you say 'Christmas Calendar'? Is it different in some way from the regular calendar?

—In fact, it is. The western Christmas calendar largely follows the liturgical calendar of the first millennium Christian Church. For a start, a 'day' can have a nonstandard meaning.

C. 1400 BOOK OF HOURS (NATIVITY DETAIL), MADE FOR JOHANNETE RAVENELLE OF PARIS [UNIVERSITY OF UPPSALA]

2. That sounds complicated.

—It's not really, but to understand why certain things are done on certain days (even to know why some people think the season of Christmas lasts for forty days) it is helpful to know something about the calendar of the early Christian church. It explains things.

**3. Now that you mention it, my grandmother insists on leaving up her Christmas decorations until the night of February 1st, which she calls Candlemas Eve. She says the lights and greenery cheer up the month of January, and she quotes some poem that says it was traditional to leave

'CANDLEMAS DAY' (MARIANNE STOKES, 1901)

them up until then. Is she right about all that?

—Believe it or not, she is. The poem she's referring to is probably Robert Herrick's *Hesperides* (published in 1648, and quoted from below) which described a world in which Christmas was assumed to last until Candlemas. The vigil of Candlemas (February 1st) was the night for taking down decorations and Candlemas Day (February 2nd) was when the burning of that year's Yule log (brand) ended, but with the remnants of it kept safe (for protection during the year, and to start next year's fire):

Chapter 2

The Christmas Calendar —The 40 Days

CEREMONIES UPON CANDLEMASS EVE (FEBRUARY 1):
    Down with the Rosemary and so
        Down with the Baies and Mistletoe;
    Down with the Holly, Ivie, all
        Wherewith ye dress the Christmas Hall;
    That so the superstitious find
        No one least branch there left behind;
    For look how many leaves there be
        Neglected there, maids, trust to me,
        So many goblins you shall see.

THE CEREMONIES FOR CANDLEMASS DAY (FEBRUARY 2):
    Kindle the Christmas brand, and then
        Till sunne-set let it burne;
    Which quencht, then lay it up agen
        Till Christmas next returne.

'WOMEN LIGHTING THE YULE LOG' (A. BARBER, *HARPER'S WEEKLY*, 1890)

>   Part must be kept wherewith to teend
>   The Christmas log next yeare,
>   And where 'tis safely kept, the fiend
>   Can do no mischiefe there.

And finally—

>   UPON CANDLEMAS DAY (FEBRUARY 2):
>   End now the white loafe and the pye,
>   And let all sports with Christmas dye.

4. And that really was normal?

LUCIE HÖFLICH AS VIOLA IN *TWELFTH NIGHT* (BERLIN, 1907)

Yes. It still is in Mexico, where Candlemas Day is a huge holiday, marking the official end of Christmas. Interestingly, Shakespeare's play *Twelfth Night* had its first performance in 1602 *not* on 5th January (Twelfth Night) but on Candlemas Eve (1st February)—as a celebratory end to the Christmas Season.

5. I'm not even sure what Candlemas Day is.

—A lot of people aren't any more. It is an important religious holiday, however.

6. What does it have to do with Christmas?

THE PRESENTATION (FRA ANGELICO C. 1440)

—It commemorates a significant milestone in the babyhood of Jesus—his presentation by Mary in the Temple (in accordance with Jewish tradition) 40 days after his birth, when her 'purification' period had ended. This is how an old carol sums up the relationship between Candlemas and Christmas:

>   On the XL *[fortieth]* Day came Mary mild,
>   Unto the temple with her child,
>   To show her clean that never was defiled,
>   And therewith endeth Christmas.

7. So was it just very religious people who celebrated Christmas until February?

—Definitely not. This perceptive verse from 18th century Williamsburg, Virginia, gives an idea of the widespread desire to extend (very secular) Christmas celebrations until Candlemas:
> Some people stretch it further yet,
>   At Candlemas they finish it.
> The gentry carry it further still
>   And finish it just when they will;
> They drink good wine and eat good cheer
>   And keep their Christmas all the year.

Chapter 2

The Christmas Calendar —The 40 Days

GOING TO A CHRISTMAS PARTY IN THE 18th CENTURY [LIT BY 'FLARING LINKS'] (*I.L.N.*, 1877)

8. I see.

—It seems that most people just liked the fun, feasting, and cheer of Christmas, and did not want it to end any sooner than it had to. This is a 1725 account by a Church of England curate, Henry Bourne:
> With some, Christmas ends with the Twelve Days, but with the generality…not till Candlemas. Till then they continue Feasting, and are ambitious of keeping some of their Christmas-Chear…

< 'CHRISTMAS GAMBOLS' (*THE WIT'S MAGAZINE*, 1784)

'COSY OLD MAIDS' CHRISTMAS' (*ILLUSTRATED LONDON NEWS*, 1889)

9. Was Candlemas a time for having Christmas parties?

—Yes. Some of the most extravagant Christmas parties (and in the world of London's lawyers, some of the strangest) were held at Candlemas.

10. What do you mean 'some of the strangest'?

—This is a description of 17th century Candlemas celebrations at Lincoln's Inn in London, one of the four Inns of Court, to which judges and barristers belong (another being Gray's Inn, *illustrated following*) and which have the right to train barristers and call them to the bar. It was written in 1852 by an English antiquarian (and lawyer) William Sandys:

(J. LEECH, 1847)

> …there was a freedom in dancing … which would scarcely suit the present day, though it would attract a considerable number of spectators to see the barristers, dressed in their best, singing and

(L. RICHTER, LEIPZIG C.1855)

dancing before the chancellor, judges, and benchers, and that on penalty of being disbarred; a threat absolutely held out, in the time of James the First, at Lincoln's Inn, because they did not dance on Candlemas Day, according to the ancient order of the Society, and some were indeed put out of commons by decimation. Imagine an unfortunate suitor inquiring about a

'THE DANCING MASTER' (J.GILLRAY, 1782)

Chapter 2

The Christmas Calendar —The 40 Days

GRAY'S INN BARRISTERS PERFORM IN 17th CENTURY COSTUME IN 1887 (*I.L.N.*, 1887)

favourite counsel, who had his case at his fingers' ends, and being told he was disbarred because he had refused to dance the night before with his opponent's counsel, the benchers not having taken into consideration the difficulty of a little man, as he was, polk-ing with a fat barrister, gown and wig and all.

11. **And that's really true?**

—Who could make it up?

12. **O.K.**

(*I.L.N.*, 1883)

—But that's not all. He goes on to quote a 17th century authority (Sir William Dugdale's *Origines Juridiciales*) which describes how the barristers' Candlemas parties involved obligatory individual singing as well as group dancing (to be continued into the night, it seemed, until the observing judges got tired of watching):

> ... one of the gentlemen of the utter barr is chosen to sing a song to the judges, sergeants, or masters of the bench; which is usually performed; and in default thereof there may be an amerciament. Then the judges and benchers take their place, and sit down at the upper end of the hall. Which done, the utter barristers and inner barristers perform a solemn revel before them. Which ended, the utter barristers take their places and sit down. Some of the gentlemen of the inner bar do present the house with dancing, which is called the post-revels, and continue their dances till the judges or bench think meet to rise and depart.

'THE BENCH' (*ENGR.* WM. HOGARTH C.1758)

13. O.K. I agree. Those were strange parties. But when did people in general stop regarding Candlemas Day as part of Christmas?

—Many still regard it way—particularly those (mostly Catholics) who have always set up a Christmas crib or manger (French *crèche*, Italian *presepio*, German *Krippe*). By tradition, the Christmas crib was left up in houses until Candlemas Day, and the three wise men not introduced until January 6th. This is a good example of how much-loved traditions establish roots, and can't be changed, even when the church that set them up makes changes.

'NOËL: LA JOLIE CRÈCHE' (*LE PETIT ECHO DE LA MODE*, 1935)

14. What do you mean?

—In the late 20th century, the Catholic Church shocked much of its congregation by shortening its liturgical season of Christmas, advancing its end from Candlemas Day to a moveable date in January. The changes, however, did not affect popular customs—as in Mexico.

Chapter 2

The Christmas Calendar —The 40 Days

15. Why?

—Many traditional Catholics believe that the feast of the Presentation of Jesus (on the 40th day after his birth) cannot be thought CRIB (A.VonKRELING, GERMANY C.1850) of as anything but part of Christmas. So if a house puts up a crib at all, there's a fair chance it's going to be left up in accordance with the childhood traditions of past generations—i.e. until 2nd February.

16. And as a secular tradition, how long did people keep celebrating Christmas until Candlemas?

—Some of the best records are from England, and there it appears to have lasted as a secular tradition until nearly the 20th century:

CHRISTMAS ROOM (ENGR. ASHBEE & DANGERFIELD 1852)

> … in some English country places it was customary, even in the late nineteenth century, to leave Christmas decorations up in houses and churches till that day (Candlemas).
> [—*Christmas in Ritual & Tradition*, Miles, 1912]

In Jane Austen's time (1775–1817), the school

Keeping Christmas Well

DANCING, 1805
'LA TRENIS'
(FROM: *LE BON GENRE*, PARIS)

Christmas holiday (including in her father's small school) continued until Candlemas. One pupil who did not return at Candlemas, but lingered at home to enjoy the 'season of dances' was sent a witty reminder of his tardiness by Jane Austen's mother, Cassandra:

> That you dance very well
>   All beholders can tell
> For lightly and nimbly you tread;
>   But pray, is it meet
>   To indulge thus your feet,
> And neglect all the while your poor head?

JANE AUSTEN'S MOTHER

'COMING HOME FROM SCHOOL FOR CHRISTMAS' (R. SEYMOUR, 1836)

'RETURNING TO SCHOOL AFTER CHRISTMAS HOLIDAYS' (R. SEYMOUR 1836)

17. But 40 days of Christmas? It sounds so unfamiliar. I always thought there were 'Twelve Days.'

—There were/are three important traditional seasons of Christmas. All of them started as dates in the church calendar, but acquired much broader significance, even in civil law.

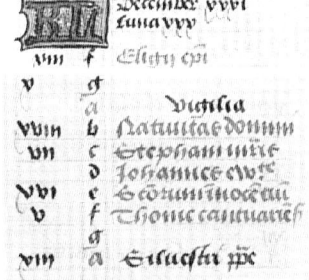

BOOK OF HOURS CALENDAR *['KL.']* DECEMBER EXTRACTS, INCL. *'NATIVITAS DOMINI'* & *'VIGILIA'*, FLANDERS c. 1460 [UNIV. OF GLASGOW]

Chapter 2

The Christmas Calendar —The 40 Days

18. Do these include days before Christmas?

—No. There are also seasons before Christmas: Advent, the Novena of Christmas (starting on December 16th), and even the nearly two months starting at All Hallows Eve, but these are considered separately.

The three seasons I'm referring to, however, are the 'Seasons of Christmas'—when Christmas had properly begun, and before it had definitively ended. On waking each morning, you were entitled to say to yourself if you wanted:

'This is a day of Christmas.'

'A PRIVATE VIEW'(J.A. FITZGERALD, *ILLUSTRATED LONDON NEWS*, 1865)

19. O.K. What are the three Seasons?

—They are:
the Forty *Days* of Christmas (from dusk on 24th December through 2nd February); the Twenty *Days* of Christmas (from dusk on 24th December through 13th January); and the Twelve *Days* of Christmas, which start a day later than the other two seasons, and extend from dusk on 25th December through 6th January. The last of these seasons is both the most significant (the 'core' of Christmas) and the most confusing (in dates). Incidentally, you will note the emphasis on the word *'Days'*.

C.1430 BELGIUM, *'COLLINS'* BOOK OF HOURS: NATIVITY
[PA. MUSEUM, U.S.]

20. Yes. Why the emphasis on *'Days'*?

—Because the 'Days of Christmas' are not ordinary days. They are not midnight to midnight days. Each 'Day of Christmas' straddles two modern calendar days.

21. What?

BOOK OF HOURS: NATIVITY IN THE *TRÈS BELLES HEURES* OF THE DUC DU BERRY (1382-1408, FRANCE)

—It's a Biblical thing. The Book of Genesis said: *'there was evening and there was morning: one day,'* so according to Biblical guidelines, the evening (not the morning) is the start of the day. In the liturgical calendar, Sundays and other holy days (such as Christmas) start on the evening of the preceding day (which is the day's Vigil or Eve). Also, a liturgical day may be longer or shorter than 24 hours.

Books of Hours

Illustrations from Books of Hours appear throughout this book. For anyone who has not come across them before, Books of Hours are medieval devotional texts—very small, and often beautifully illuminated. They were much in demand in an age when prayer took up a large part of the day and night—not only for monks, but also for lay people, who wanted to pray to the monks' pattern.

NATIVITY PAGE, FLANDERS C. 1460

An 'Hour' refers to the Liturgy of the Hours or the Divine Office, a fixed compendium of devotions/prayers (varying from day to day) to be performed at prescribed times of the natural day and night:

VESPERS [BEFORE SUNSET]; **COMPLINE** [BEFORE RETIRING];
MATINS [DURING THE NIGHT]; **LAUDS** [SUNRISE];
PRIME [FIRST HOUR OF THE DAY]; **TERCE** [THIRD HOUR OF THE DAY];
SEXT [SIXTH HOUR OF THE DAY (OR, MID-DAY)];
NONE [NINTH HOUR OF THE DAY (OR MID-AFTERNOON)].

For lay people, this was a lot of praying, but for monks, praying was (and maybe is) almost constant, and the battle against sleepiness was not one they always won. Hence the children's nursery song:

*Frère Jacques, Frère Jacques, dormez-vous ? Dormez-vous ?
Sonnez les Matines ! Sonnez les Matines ! ... ...'*

71

Chapter 2

The
Christmas
Calendar
—The 40
Days

ABOVE RIGHT & BOTTOM RIGHT: NATIVITY AND EPIPHANY IMAGES FROM A FLANDERS BOOK OF HOURS C.1460 [GLASGOW UNIVERSITY]

MIDDLE RIGHT > : NATIVITY FROM *THE 'DE GREY' HOURS* MADE IN FLANDERS C.1450 FOR THE ENGLISH MARKET (OF SARUM USE) [NAT. LIB. WALES]

BELOW LEFT: THE EARLIEST WESTERN NATIVITY IMAGE, C. 800 AD, IS IN THE ILLUMINATED GOSPELS TEXT *THE BOOK OF KELLS*, IRELAND

22. Again, what?

—This means that the important holy day (or 'solemnity') that is Christmas begins at dusk on the 24th of December.

23. You mean Christmas *Day* begins at dusk on the 24th of December?

GOING TO CHRISTMAS EVE SERVICES IN NORWAY
(L.J. BRIDGMAN, 1916)

—In effect, yes, as the evening is the start of the day.

24. That's a bit confusing. Is it just at Christmas that the night is regarded as the first part of the day?

—No. That's how the liturgical calendar works all year round for holy days. It's why Catholics, for instance, can attend a Sunday Mass on Saturday evening—because by the liturgical calendar, Saturday evening is Sunday. (A word for Saturday in German, introduced by St Boniface, is *Sonnabend*: 'the evening of Sunday'.)

PETRIKIRCHE ON CHRISTMAS EVE
[*- AM HEILIGEN ABEND'*] MÜHLHAUSEN, GERMANY (C. MICHEL, 1860)

25. In fact, that's more than a bit confusing. It's very confusing.

Chapter 2

The Christmas Calendar —The 40 Days

—It is now, but it wasn't in the past. Right through the 18th century, you would see the Twelve Eves (or Nights) of Christmas referred to separately from the Twelve Days of Christmas. Records of Henry VIII's reign describe the night of 6th January (an occasion for elaborate Christmas pageants and masques) as *'the daie of the Epiphanie at nyghte'* [—Sandys]. And everyone knew about the Vigils of Sundays or holy days, whether they were for them or against them.

'A MOTHER ON CHRISTMAS EVE'
(L. RICHTER, GERMANY, 1851)

26. Um …

—Maybe we should start at the beginning. Not much about the Twelve Days' season is straightforward, but when you know how and why it came into being, it is easier to understand. We'll look at it in detail in chapter 4, after an interlude chapter.

NATIVITY SCENE WITH WASHING LINE

(L. RICHTER, DRESDEN, C. 1850)

CHAPTER 3

—*Interlude*—
The Tom and Jerry

...many people think Christmas is invented only to furnish an excuse for hot Tom and Jerry. [—Damon Runyon, *Guys and Dolls*]

'...ANY NUTMEG IN THIS SILLY HOUSE?—I'M MAKING TOM AND JERRYS.'—*THE CHEATERS*, 1945

'...the tree is up, and the Tom and Jerry mix is in the refrigerator.'   [—*The Apartment*, 1960]

'What'll you have lad? —I'm having Tom and Jerry myself. ... Get a Tom and Jerry for the young lady, George.'
[—*Beyond Tomorrow*, 1940]

There are so many Christmas drinks, you may wonder why we highlight the Tom and Jerry. A very old cocktail (from London in 1821) *[see note at end of chapter]*, it was once a Christmas mainstay in the US, often served in special sets—a large bowl and mugs with the words 'Tom and Jerry' printed on them.

The Tom and Jerry was hit hard by Prohibition, but regained its ground as a traditional Christmas drink in the 1930s, 40s, and 50s. It is said to have faded from popularity largely because it was considered a troublesome drink to make.

So why are we giving a recipe just for this drink? Damon Runyon *[right >]* is the answer, and his very funny Christmas short story, *Dancing Dan's Christmas*.

DAYMON RUNYON (CENTRE) IN A NEW YORK BAR IN 1944

We challenge anyone who reads *Dancing Dan's Christmas* (and everyone should) to restrain themselves from searching out the rum and the eggs before they even finish the story. Much of the action takes place in a New York speakeasy on Christmas Eve with characters giving their all to drinking hot Tom and Jerrys and singing the praises of the drink (made of necessity, because of Prohibition, with drugstore rye which the proprietor, Charley Bernstein, has got on prescription for his rheumatism).

It is explained that the Tom and Jerry was a traditional drink, so popular before Prohibition that 'many people think Christmas is invented only to

TOM & JERRY PREPARATION IN *BEYOND TOMORROW*, 1940

Chapter 3

Interlude

The Tom and Gerry

furnish an excuse for hot Tom and Jerry.' When rum could no longer be got, people gave up on the drink because 'making Tom and Jerry is by no means child's play.'

TOM & JERRYS IN *THE CHEATERS*, 1945

In fact it is not that hard a drink to make, but in order to make the exercise worthwhile, there are a few essentials to remember—

First of all, do not even consider making this drink with hot water (although some recipes might suggest it). Make it with hot milk. It is really *not* a very nice drink made with hot water, but it is a gorgeous one made with hot milk. (And by hot, we mean very hot—near the boil.) If you are making a large amount in a bowl, heat the bowl first. Also, warm your mugs and have the bottles of brandy and rum at room temperature. It is important to use the freshest of eggs, preferably free-range and organic. And be generous with the spices—and with the liquor! It is Christmas! Regarding quantities: One large egg beaten will make five Tom and Jerrys. The amount of spirits needed is listed per serving. To make a large batch, adjust amounts from the basic recipe below. (A 700 ml bottle of rum will make 16 Tom and Jerrys; the brandy goes exactly twice as far.)

The following is our favourite recipe:

Chapter 3

Interlude

The Tom and Gerry

1 egg separated,
one tsp. powdered sugar (per egg),
1 jigger* dark rum (per serving),
½ jigger* cognac (per serving),
very generous pinches (at least ⅛ tsp. each)
    ground allspice, cinnamon, cloves, nutmeg,
hot milk.

[* 1 jigger = 44 ml. = 1½ fluid ounces]

Beat the yolk very thoroughly with the sugar and spices. Beat the egg white until very stiff, and add to the yolk mix.

To make individual drinks, pour two tablespoons of this mix into a warmed mug [of approx. 6 oz (175 ml) size].

Add the rum and the cognac. Top up with very hot milk and sprinkle with nutmeg.

[Repeat as necessary]

A note on the name— The term *'Tom and Jerry'* comes from characters in a very popular book of 1821 by Pierce Egan, on the adventures of Regency men-about-town: *Life in London, or the Day and Night Scenes of Jerry Hawthorn Esq. and his Elegant Friend, Corinthian Tom.* In order to publicise the book (and a stage play developed from it) Egan invented the *'Tom and Jerry.'*

'CORINTHIAN CAPITAL'.
FROM EGAN'S *DAY AND NIGHT SCENES OF TOM AND JERRY—UPS AND DOWNS OF LIFE IN LONDON* (FRONTISPIECE: R+G.CRUIKSHANK, 1821)

CHAPTER 4
The Traditional but Surprising Christmas Calendar:

The Twelve Days of Christmas

1. So when exactly are the Twelve Days of Christmas?

—Be warned. The answer might be surprising to modern Christmas-keepers. They are the Twelve Days *after* the commemoration of the Nativity. (Also, as mentioned, they are not all equal 24-hour days, but we'll come to that later.)

2. Hold on. That would mean Christmas Day is *not* one of the Twelve Days of Christmas?

—Correct. The *Day* of December 25th is *not* the First of the Twelve Days of Christmas. However, the *night* of December 25th is the First of the Twelve Nights of Christmas (or the first of the Twelve Eves of Christmas).

3. But that's ridiculous. What about Christmas Eve? Isn't that the first Eve of Christmas?

—I said the Twelve Days were bewildering. They

'CHRISTMAS EVE' (*HARPER'S WEEKLY*, 1889)

first arose in a specific historic context (in Rome, in the fourth century)—the time when, and the place where, the Christmas we now know came into being.

4. But why Twelve Days?

—Because in the fourth century, the church in Rome (but not outside Rome) changed the date on which it celebrated the birth of Christ from January 6th to December 25th. This change was not without controversy. The Twelve Days linked the (new) December date and the (old) January date.

FOURTH CENTURY SARCOPHAGUS, ST AGNES' CEMETERY, ROME: GIFTS OF THE MAGI (ONE OF THE EARLIEST REPRESENTATIONS OF THE NATIVITY)

5. Is there any record of this?

—Yes. There is a written reference in an interesting document of 354 AD: an illustrated calendar, drawn by an artist named Philocalus for a wealthy Roman named Valentinus. The calendar (a Renaissance copy of which *[below]* is in the Vatican Library) makes this evocative statement:

VIII KAL. IAN. NATUS CHRISTUS IN BETLEEM IUDEAE. [—Eight days before the Kalends of January (i.e. on December 25th) Christ was born in Bethlehem of Judea.]

CALENDAR OF PHILOCALUS, 354 AD, COVER PAGE [COPY C.1604, ORIGINAL LOST]

This 354 AD document incorporated a lost

Chapter 4

The Christmas Calendar —The 12 Days

document of 336 AD, and it is thought that this earlier year was when the change to the December date was made.

6. But you say this change of date was controversial?

—Yes. Outside of Rome, the Christian Church was not quick to accept it. The Church in Constantinople accepted it only in about 380 AD; the Church in Antioch in 388 AD; the church in Alexandria in 432 AD; and the Church in Jerusalem in the 7th century. The Church in Armenia *never* accepted it, and still celebrates the Nativity on January 6th.

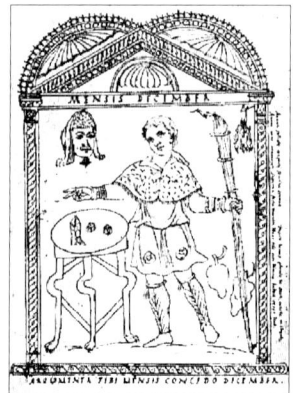

CALENDAR OF PHILOCALUS, 354 AD, PAGE FOR MONTH OF DECEMBER WITH DICE-TABLE, MASK, FOOD … [BARBERINI COPY 1620, ORIG. LOST]

7. Um…

—Well, more about that later. The important bit is that it was during this period, when there were strong opposing feelings within the Christian Church about whether December 25th or January 6th should be the date for commemorating the Nativity, that a written reference to Christmas as an official Church Season (rather than a single day) appears. Have you heard of the pretty term 'Festal Tide'?

'COUNTRY CHURCH, CHRISTMAS MORNING' (R. SEYMOUR, ENGLAND, 1836)

8. No. What does it mean?

—As a church term, it means that a feast is to be recognized as a season, and not just as a single day. This is Webster's definition:

> 'Festal Tide': A point or period of time, as in a day, year or lifetime; a definite moment, period, season, or occasion; esp. an ecclesiastical anniversary; a festival or, often, *its season as distinguished from the day on which it falls.*

Chapter 4

The Christmas Calendar —The 12 Days

The first known reference to the Twelve Days of Christmas as a 'Festal Tide' appeared at the end of the fourth century, and the Twelve Days were officially declared a Festal Tide by the second Council of Tours in the sixth century.

(VIZETELLY, 1851, CHRISTMAS WITH THE POETS)

9. Um … another strange term there—Council of Tours.

—O.K. The Council of Tours ('Tours' being the town in France) was a church Council—i.e. 'an assembly of ecclesiastics convened to consider matters of doctrine, discipline, law or morals' [—*Webster*]. Church Councils feature prominently in any history of Christmas. It has already been noted that St Nicholas attended the fourth-century Council of Nicea (in present-day Turkey). The 20th century 'Vatican II' was a church Council.

CHRISTMAS BELLS (DETAIL FROM: *CHRISTMAS IN ART & SONG*, J.A. HOWS, 1879)

10. O.K.

—The history (along with the magic) of the

Keeping Christmas Well

Twelve Days was summarized neatly in an intelligent, heartfelt book about Christmas published in 1912:

> ...it will be well to glance at the character of the Twelve Days as a whole, and at the superstitions which hang around the season. So many are these superstitions, so 'bewitched' is the time, that the older mythologists not unnaturally saw in it a Teutonic festal season, dating from the pre-Christian days. In point of fact, it appears to be simply a creation of the Church, a natural linking together of Christmas and Epiphany [January 6th]. It is first mentioned as a festal tide by the eastern Father, Ephræm Syrus, at the end of the fourth century, and was declared to be such by the western Council of Tours in 567. [— *Christmas in Ritual and Tradition*, Miles, 1912]

EPHRAEM SYRUS (4th CENTURY AD)

THE EPIPHANY (L. RICHTER, DRESDEN, C.1850)

11. So the Twelve Days really meant something? I wouldn't even have heard of them if it weren't for the song.

CHRISTMAS ISLAND STAMPS OF 1977, DEPICTING LYRICS OF *12 DAYS OF CHRISTMAS*

Chapter 4

The Christmas Calendar —The 12 Days

—A lot of people say that now, but in the past, i.e. before the Industrial Revolution, everyone who celebrated Christmas (which was most of the Western Christian world, except for a few Calvinist hot-spots) celebrated it as a season that did not even begin to wind down until the night of January 6th. Those who could (particularly the rich) might celebrate until Candlemas, but even the poor (notably farm labourers) were saved from having to make too rapid a transition back to the world of work after the long Christmas.

ST DISTAFF'S DAY (*CHAMBERS' BOOK OF DAYS*, 1869)

12. What do you mean?

—Well, January 7th was St Distaff's Day, which, according to the poet Robert Herrick, was a transitional day between Christmas and the return to working life—an occasion for 'partly work and partly play.' [And no, there is no St Distaff. The day was named after the traditional tool for spinning—a job which women resumed, but with hearty rustic diversions (according to Herrick) to ease their return to work—on the day after the Twelve-Day Season had ended.] Men did not return fully to work until the Monday after January 6th—Plough Monday.

Keeping Christmas Well

SPIRIT OF THE SEASON (C. D. GIBSON, U.S., 1906)

BELOW: 'CHRISTMAS BELLES' (WINSLOW HOMER, *HARPER'S WEEKLY*, 1869)

13. So what about the song *Twelve Days of Christmas*—does it have any significance, and is there an explanation for the lyrics?

—If the song did not exist, most people would no longer know that there is a Twelve-Days' Season of Christmas—that is now its main significance. As for the lyrics, no one is sure what the explanation of them is. Most say the song is either French or English in origin. It dates back to at least the 18th century, because it featured in an English children's book of 1780, *Mirth Without Mischief [right >]*, but it (or a similar song) might date from as early as the 13th century. There are theories about the list of presents, which varied a bit with

time and place. Some of the wilder theories give them a religious significance, suggesting they amounted to a code language for Catholics when Catholicism was suppressed in England; others say that its lyrics were the basis for a memory game, particularly one played by children (both in England and France) on Twelfth Night.

Chapter 4

The Christmas Calendar —The 12 Days

TWELFTH NIGHT CHILDREN'S PARTY GAMES (*PEARS ANNUAL*, 1896)

14 So the lyrics don't really mean anything?

—Hard to say. Although the lyrics—i.e. the list of gifts—are perplexing now, it is interesting how often 'pipers piping' and 'drummers drumming' are referred to in historical accounts of English 'Lord of Misrule' parades. Swans were a Christmas dish for the rich; and whatever about 'lords a-leaping' at Christmas, we have already noted how English lawyers were obliged to do sustained leaping at parties to mark the end of Christmas. Whether any of this inspired the lyrics or not, no one knows.

CHRISTMAS ISLAND, INDIAN OCEAN (DISCOVERED CHRISTMAS DAY, 1643): *TWELVE DAYS OF CHRISTMAS* STAMPS 1977

EPIPHANY (LUDWIG RICHTER, GERMANY, C. 1860)

BELOW: MADONNA AND CHILD (LUDWIG RICHTER, GERMANY, C. 1860)

15. Am I right in thinking that, at one time, the whole Twelve-Days Season had as much importance as December 25th has now, and was a really long public holiday?

—It seems the Twelve Days were about that important. Certainly the significance of the Season extended beyond the church and affected civil life and laws:

> In England, in the days of King Alfred, the Twelve Days finishing on January 6th were made Festivals. [—Bourne]
>
> Some writers are of the opinion that, but for Alfred's strict observance of the 'full twelve holy days' he would not have been defeated by the Danes in the year 878. [Dawson]

CHRISTMAS EVE TRUCE OF 1914 (*I.L.N.*, JAN. 1915)

16. That was unfortunate.

—King Alfred was not alone in losing a battle because he was a good Christmas-keeper. It seems that German devotion to Christmas may have helped Americans to win their War of Independence. The soldiers (on the British side) whom George Washington fought after he crossed the Delaware on Christmas night 1776 were from Hesse in Germany. It is said to have been an advantage to the Americans that the Hessian soldiers were preoccupied because of Christmas. A note warning that the Americans were approaching had been brought to their commander, Colonel Rahl, on Christmas Eve when he was having his dinner. He apparently ignored the note, was fatally wounded in the battle the next day, and the note was found in his pocket.

Chapter 4

The Christmas Calendar —The 12 Days

SURRENDER OF HESSIAN TROOPS TO GENL. GEORGE WASHINGTON, CHRISTMAS 1776 (1850 LITHOGRAPH)

CHRISTMAS 1914: 'BRITISH AND GERMAN SOLDIERS ARM-IN-ARM EXCHANGING FOOD & GIFTS' (A.C. MICHAEL, *I.L.N.*)

17. There's one thing bothering me about those 'Twelve' days…

—O.K. but first let me mention a final bit of history about them because it was a pretty development and showed how significant that 'Twelve-Days' Festal Tide was—how everyone took for granted that Christmas was to be celebrated as a season, rather than just as a single day:

The laws of Ethelred II (991-1016) and of Edward the Confessor ordained it [the Festal

Keeping Christmas Well

PHOTO, YPRES-ARMENTIÈRE, 1914: BRITISH & GERMAN SOLDIERS MEET ON CHRISTMAS DAY (*ILLUSTRATED WAR NEWS*, JANUARY 1915) DESCRIBED IN THE FOLLOWING LONDON SOLDIER'S LETTER HOME—

'...SOON AFTER DUSK ON THE 24th THE GERMANS PUT UP LANTERNS ON THE TOP OF THEIR TRENCHES AND STARTED SINGING... FIRING CEASED ON BOTH SIDES, AND BOTH GERMANS AND ENGLISH VENTURED OUT. ...AFTER DAYBREAK ON CHRISTMAS DAY SMALL PARTIES ON BOTH SIDES VENTURED OUT, ALL UNARMED. ...WHEN I AND SOME PALS STROLLED UP FROM THE RESERVE TRENCHES AFTER DINNER, WE FOUND A CROWD OF SOME HUNDRED TOMMIES OF EACH NATIONALITY BETWEEN THE TRENCHES. ONE OF THE GERMANS HAD BEEN A WAITER AT THE SAVOY; AND ANOTHER A WEST-END BARBER'S ASSISTANT. TALK AND SOUVENIRS WERE EXCHANGED...'

'CHRISTMAS IN A TRENCH' GERMANY 1914 (*ARTIST UNKNOWN*)

Chapter 4

The Christmas Calendar —The 12 Days

ABOVE: '*AM HEILIGEN ABEND*' —'ON CHRISTMAS EVE 1914,' - GERMAN SOLDIERS RIDE PAST A CHURCH (L. KOCH, GERMANY, 1915)

Christmas in Wartime

< *LEFT:* '*LES MARTYRS DE L'ARRIÈRE*' —'MARTYRS OF THE HOME FRONT' (COVER IMAGE FROM *LE RIRE* MAGAZINE, FRANCE, 1916)

BELOW: '*WIGILJA W ZIEMIANCE*' —'CHRISTMAS EVE IN A DUGOUT' - POLISH SOLDIERS IN W.W.I, WITH CHRISTMAS TREE (S. PLEWINSKA, POSTCARD C. 1915)

Keeping Christmas Well

Tide of the Twelve Days] to be a time of peace and concord among Christian men, when all strife must cease. [Chambers, 1903; *also* Miles, 1912]

18. That's all very interesting, but while you have been going through this history, I have been doing arithmetic. Unless you say that Christmas Day is not part of Christmas at all, it means there are really Thirteen Days of Christmas rather than Twelve Days of Christmas?

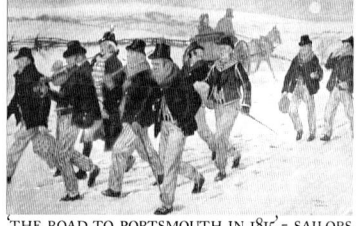

'THE ROAD TO PORTSMOUTH IN 1815' – SAILORS ENDING CHRISTMAS LEAVE (*THE GRAPHIC*, 1915)

—In fact, that's true, but thirteen days are not spoken of much. It has been speculated, believe it or not, that the church did not want to acknowledge a season of thirteen days, and that is why it declared the 26th to be the first of the Twelve Days.

19. Who speculated?

—There are a few interesting references to the problematic status of a 13-day season by 18th and 19th century authors. In 1725, for instance, Henry Bourne quoted this description of King Arthur's Christmas by the 16th century historian Hector Bœthius (not because he considered the information about Arthur to be factually reliable, but as an indication of how ancient the 'abuse' of the

KING ARTHUR'S CHRISTMAS (J. GILBERT, 1865)

Christmas festival was):

> That King Arthur kept with his Nobles at York a very prophane Christmas for Thirteen Days together, and that such Jollity and Feasting then had its Original from him.

Re-quoting this passage, Bourne explained in 1725 (and remember that we mentioned above that there are three traditional seasons of Christmas: 40 days, 20 days, and 12 days):

> Christmas Day is said to be none of the twelve days. For if it was added, it would make them thirteen days, which are the Thirteen Days here mentioned. It is said to be among the Twenty Days, because, as I imagine, it was reckon'd among those twenty Days in which the Church forbad Fasting.

20. I see.

'THE MONK'S REPAST' (W.D. SADLER 1854-1923)

—A mid-nineteenth century antiquarian appeared to have reached the same conclusion: that the only purpose in calling the season Twelve Days was to be able to avoid calling it Thirteen Days:

> ...in the old Runic festivals, among the ancient Danes, it [January 6th] appears to have been more correctly called the thirteenth day, *a name which would sound uncouth to our modern ears.* [—Sandys, 1852]

21. You know, I have really never heard of the Twenty Days of Christmas.

DETAIL 'CHRISTMAS ON THE LONDON UNDERGROUND' (*THE SPHERE*, 1902)

—O.K. In chapter 6, the Twenty Days of Christmas—after an interlude chapter.

Chapter 4

The Christmas Calendar —The 12 Days

CHAPTER 5

—*Interlude*—
Scrooge Movies

Not everyone has read *A Christmas Carol* (a quick, fun read), but is there anyone who has not seen a filmed adaptation of it?

Scrooge Movies—Traditional

A Christmas Carol has been turned into more than a hundred films, either for the cinema or for television, and the story never loses its appeal.

The following are classic, traditional adaptations (those set in 19th century London, and with venerable actors playing Scrooge)—

SOL EYTINGE, *A CHRISTMAS CAROL*, BOSTON, 1869
(EYTINGE IMAGES SCANNED BY PHILIP V. ALLINGHAM, *SEE 'SOURCES'*)

Chapter 5

Scrooge Movies

Traditional

A CHRISTMAS CAROL, 1935, WITH SEYMOUR HICKS (who had previously played the role of Scrooge in a silent film in 1913, and who co-wrote this screenplay). Hicks is a grumpy, convincing Scrooge. Because he is an unfamiliar actor now, it's easy to think that he *is* Scrooge. Everything about his appearance says miser: he is unkempt, uncombed, and lives in rooms that look as shabby as his haircut. The London in this film is the foggy, dark city described in the book; and the obviously necessary 'flaring links' that Dickens describes (torches to light a person on his way through the streets), which are ignored in other adaptations, are shown in this one.

A CHRISTMAS CAROL, 1938, WITH REGINALD OWEN. Not greatly admired, although it is entertaining if you are not a devotee of the book. In this adaptation, the London of the 1840s is a brightly lit city of well-dressed people, and even the impoverished Cratchits appear plump and prosperous. The wonderfully portly Gene Lockhart *[below]* plays Bob Cratchit.

BOB CRATCHIT
(S. EYTINGE,
< 1869)

A CHRISTMAS CAROL, 1951, WITH ALASTAIR SIM. A highly regarded adaptation (and Alastair's Sim's performance is brilliant) but some lovers of Dickens have reservations about the script, which departed from a central tenet of Dickens's book: that a selfish disregard for others is all that is required for damnation.

For many readers, this is the magic of his story—that it is not necessary to be dishonest, or actively to do harm, to end up in Dickens's interesting hell (in which moaning businessmen are chained forever to safes and cash-boxes). All you have to do is to fail to help those whose lives you might have made better.

In the book, being cold-hearted (even if honest) was enough to seal your fate, but in this film, outright villainy is required. The script has Scrooge leave the kind Fezziwig's employ to work for a man who turns out to be an embezzler; and then he and Marley are able to take over the embezzler's business. Ultimately (although it is not clear how this happens) Scrooge and Marley are seen to put poor Fezziwig himself out of business.

MARLEY & SCROOGE (S. EYTINGE, 1869)

Still the film has extraordinary moments. One

of the great evocative lines in the book describes Scrooge's Christmas Eve dinner:

> Scrooge took his melancholy dinner in his usual melancholy tavern; and having read all the newspapers, and beguiled the rest of the evening with his banker's-book, went home to bed.

In the film, Scrooge asks the waiter for more bread. The waiter tells him it will be a ha'penny extra. Scrooge's wish for the bread vies with impossibility of paying the extra money, and finally he tells the waiter he won't bother. The fierce internal debate lasts only a moment, but every stage of it registers on Sim's face.

Chapter 5

Scrooge Movies

Traditional

SCROOGE REFUSES MONEY FOR CHARITY: 'THE PHILANTHROPISTS' (S. EYTINGE, BOSTON, 1869)

A Christmas Carol, 1984, WITH GEORGE C. SCOTT. Scott's performance, not surprisingly, is a towering one—his unreformed Scrooge at the beginning of the film really would frighten a blind man's dog. This adaptation is largely true to the Dickens story, but the makers still felt a need to make Scrooge less of a straight-dealer than he was in the book ('Scrooge's name was good upon 'Change for anything

'ON 'CHANGE' (EYTINGE, 1869)

he chose to put his hand to'). The scene, for instance, when Scrooge tells traders that his price for corn is 5% higher than he had offered the day before, and will be 5% higher the next day is the film's invention. The young Scrooge in this screenplay was the Scrooge of the story—a bookish little boy, depending on Ali Baba and Robinson Crusoe for company in his lonely schooldays (an interesting element in the story, but forgotten in other adaptations). This film has probably the best Tiny Tim. He is small, his voice sounds weak and innocent, and he is made to look convincingly sick.

(ENGR. BY A.V.S. ANTHONY AFTER SOL EYTINGE, EVERY SATURDAY JOURNAL, BOSTON, 1870)

ABOVE: 'TIM'S RIDE' - THE FIRST IMAGE SHOWING TINY TIM ON HIS FATHER'S SHOULDER. (SOL EYTINGE, BOSTON, 1869) [SOURCE OF 1870 ENGRAVING ABOVE]

RIGHT: A PHOTOGRAPH TAKEN IN THE 1840S OF THE 'REAL' TINY TIM—DICKENS'S SISTER FANNY'S CRIPPLED SON, HARRY BURNETT, WHO DIED IN 1849. FANNY'S PASTOR RECALLED THAT 'HARRY WAS A SINGULAR CHILD, MEDITATIVE AND QUAINT IN A SINGULAR DEGREE.' (PHOTO ORIGINALLY OWNED BY CHARLES DICKENS'S MOTHER.)
[FROM: BERG COLLECTION, NEW YORK PUBLIC LIBRARY]

Chapter 5

Scrooge Movies

Traditional

A CHRISTMAS CAROL, 1999, WITH PATRICK STEWART. Not taken as seriously as it should be, this is the favourite adaptation of many who really love the book. It depicts Dickens's Scrooge more faithfully than any of the others do (and the sets are great).

Patrick Stewart's Scrooge is a bad-tempered, selfish miser who has done nothing to make other people's lives better, but that is the full extent (and it is plenty) of his villainy. This Scrooge is thin, which is appropriate—how would a miser get fat?—and is splenetic as only a thin person can be splenetic. Stewart conveys the changing Scrooge with great sympathy and subtlety: as the reformed Scrooge on Christmas Day, he is mindful enough of the miser he used to be that he chokes slightly on the word 'shilling' which he offers to a boy as payment for fetching the poulterer. In a memorable scene near the end, Scrooge, with difficulty, re-learns how to laugh [>].

There is real respect for the book in this adaptation, and the gratuitous changes that have been introduced in other films avoided. The sister who brings Scrooge home from school at Christmas, for instance, is the young child of the book ('a little girl, much younger than the boy …').

(S. EYTINGE, 1869)

Richard E. Grant—cringing to just the right degree—is a perfect (the best ever?) Bob Cratchit, and Saskia Reeves, singing as she works, is a lively, entertaining Mrs Crachit.

SCROOGE—THE MUSICAL, 1970, WITH ALBERT FINNEY. Many raise their eyebrows at the idea of *Scrooge—the Musical*, but this movie is good fun, easy on the eye, and surprisingly true to the spirit of Dickens. Don't expect wonderful singing, but the only musical numbers you wish they might have left out are the Tiny Tim song, and the one sung by Scrooge's old girlfriend. Albert Finney (hunched and convincingly aged) is great fun to watch as Scrooge; and an appealing feature of this version (unlike any other) is that the same actor (the un-aged and very dishy Albert Finney of 1970) plays the young Scrooge.

—*And*—

THE MUPPET CHRISTMAS CAROL, 1992, STARRING MICHAEL CAINE. Tell anyone under age 25 that you are writing about Scrooge movies, and their response will be: 'Don't forget *The Muppet Christmas Carol*.' This film introduced a generation (to date) to the Dickens story. Kermit the Frog is Bob Cratchit, Miss Piggy is Mrs Cratchit, The Great Gonzo is Charles Dickens, and Michael Caine is a fine Scrooge (even the Talking Vegetables think he's mean).

Scrooge.— Let us deal with the eviction
        notices for tomorrow, Mr Cratchit.
Bob Cratchit.— Tomorrow's Christmas, Sir.
Scrooge.— Very well. You may gift-wrap them.

Scrooge Movies—Adaptations and Cartoons

Chapter 5

Scrooge Movies

Adaptations

(S. EYTINGE, 1869 FRONTISPIECE)

There have been many adaptations of *A Christmas Carol* in modern settings. The following is a short list of some of the better ones.

'MARLEY'S FACE' (SOL EYTINGE, BOSTON, 1869)

Keeping Christmas Well

A CHRISTMAS CAROL WITH ROSS KEMP (first broadcast in 2000 on ITV). Ross Kemp is the leather-jacketed loan shark, Eddie Scrooge—the terror of a poor estate in modern London. His unfortunate clients are depicted sympathetically. On Christmas Eve, he repossesses the television of a single mother. 'I'm begging you,' she says, running after him, 'We want a traditional Christmas like everyone else—that telly goes on at seven in the morning and stays on till midnight.' In response, Eddie throws her television from an upper-storey balcony. The script (by Peter Bowker) seems to have been influenced as much by *Groundhog Day* as by *A Christmas Carol*, but the combination of the two plots works very well.

The ghosts are Eddie's father ('Christmas Past'), his murdered partner Marley ('Christmas Present'), and—most effective of all—a silent child ('Christmas Yet to Come') who turns out to be his own future child. A very satisfying contemporary Christmas movie. [Unfortunately, not on DVD (or VHS) at time of writing.]

(S. EYTINGE, BOSTON, 1869)

Chapter 5

Scrooge Movies

Adaptations

SCROOGED, 1988, WITH BILL MURRAY. Some critics were unenthusiastic about this film when it was released, but they must have been very dry (or at least unreformed) people. This is an imaginative, often hilarious adaptation—not subtle, but very smart. Bill Murray (Scrooge) is Frank Cross, program chief of a television network, which is to transmit a (crazy) adaptation of *A Christmas Carol* live on Christmas Eve night (Olympic gymnast, Mary Lou Retton, is Tiny Tim). A traditional trailer has been prepared showing a dignified John Houseman ('America's favourite old fart') sitting in front of a fire and reading from Dickens, but Cross replaces this with an action sequence so frightening (it finishes with a mushroom cloud) that a woman watching suffers a heart attack. 'You can't buy publicity like this,' Cross says when he hears the news.

This version has great ghosts. The 'Marley' character (played by John Forsythe, *below*) is a television executive who died on the golf course, and who appears to Cross in rotted golf gear. Carol Kane may be the most-memorable-ever 'Ghost of Christmas Present.' With the wings, white dress and long curly hair of a good fairy, she demands Cross's attention by slapping, kicking, and smashing him in the face with a toaster. Bill Murray is so perfect as the unreformed Scrooge that you regret it when he becomes good, but that, as we know, is the story.

A DIVA'S CHRISTMAS CAROL, 2000, WITH VANESSA WILLIAMS. This is a witty, underrated adaptation from the US cable music station VH1. Vanessa Williams almost explodes from the screen as the talented but terrible diva, Ebony Scrooge, who is now a solo artist, but started out singing with two others—the dead Marli (played by Rozonda 'Chilli' Thomas *[below]* of TLC, who wears her chains with style) and Terri (who has fallen into poverty). There are nice touches in this adaptation: Ebony's childhood horror is genuinely moving—Ebony and her kind older brother live with a drunken father, and are separated when they are put into care. There is an appropriately rock-'n'-roll 'Ghost of Christmas Present' (John Taylor of Duran Duran). Occupying a room next to Ebony's in a luxury New York hotel, he is surrounded by a different kind of Christmas plenty: instead of the usual mountain of turkeys, geese and cakes, his room is filled with spaced-out, gorgeous young women. This version is remarkably true to the spirit of the book, and good fun. [On region-1 DVD (& VHS) at time of writing.]

(EYTINGE, 1869)

Chapter 5

Scrooge Movies Adaptations

EBBIE, 1995, WITH SUSAN LUCCI (sometimes called *Miracle at Christmas—Ebbie's Story*).

A made-for-television adaptation—not sophisticated, but works for family viewing. The influence of the 1951 Alastair Sim film is apparent in the script. The teenage Ebbie (Elizabeth) is given a job by a kind couple who own an American department store. Ultimately, she and a man named Marley oust the couple and take over the store.

This adaptation deals better than most with the matter of the over-sized Christmas-Day turkey delivered by Scrooge to the Cratchits. This plot development always begs the question of how Mrs Cratchit could get the big bird cooked in time (particularly as the Cratchits were dependent on a bakery to do their roasting). In this version, Ebbie goes to a Chinese delicatessen on Christmas day and buys its largest cooked turkey. [Only on VHS, at time of writing.]

'THE PRIZE TURKEY' (S. EYTINGE, BOSTON 1869)

(A. RACKHAM, 1915)

THE CHEATERS, 1945 (WITH EUGENE PALLETTE, JOSEPH SCHILDKRAUT, BILLIE BURKE & ONA MUNSON). An interesting, likeable curiosity—not billed as an adaptation of *A Christmas Carol*, but that's what it turns out to be. Except in this film, it is not the appearance of ghosts that reforms the 'cheaters' of the title, but the narrating to them of the story of *A Christmas Carol* by a down-at-heel actor (played by Schildkraut). *The Cheaters* is not well known, and although it may seem just giddy at the start, the plot develops into a nicely original film.

Set in New York in 1945, the Pidgeon family (not as rich as it used to be) follows a fashionable social practice of taking in a homeless person at Christmas. They choose the impoverished actor.

A rich relative (whose money they have been waiting to inherit) dies, but they learn he has left his money to a former child actress (Ona Munson, who played Belle Watling in *Gone With the Wind*) if she can be found 'in a reasonable time.'  The family decides to find the actress first, and prevent her learning of the will. They tell her she is a cousin (she knows she is not, but, penniless, she goes along with the story), and they take her away to spend Christmas with them in an isolated house in the country. Their servants quit, and the family, actor and actress are left to fend for themselves. On Christmas Eve night, the actor recites the plot of *A Christmas Carol*, and the story of what happened to Scrooge causes everyone to reform. The actress, Florie, says she knows she cannot be a cousin. The family admits to the her that she has inherited $5 million. The actress and the down-at-heel actor seem as if they will have a future together. Undoubtedly a Christmas plot.

MRS PIDGEON (BILLIE BURKE) STEPS OVER AN INEBRIATED UNCLE WILLIE IN HIS SANTA COSTUME, SAYING TO FLORIE (ONA MUNSON): 'WILLIE'S ALWAYS SUCH A GENTLEMAN.'

[Unfortunately not available on DVD (or VHS) at time of writing, but is sometimes rebroadcast at Christmas.]

SCROOGE MOVIES—CARTOONS

MICKEY'S CHRISTMAS CAROL, 1983, WITH SCROOGE MCDUCK. This appealing cartoon runs for less than half an hour, but makes you laugh a lot in that time. The artwork is pure Disney rather than Dickens, but is charming. The film was nominated for an Oscar, and it marked the return to movies after 30 years of Mickey Mouse (playing Bob Cratchit).

Scrooge Movies—Cartoons

A Christmas Carol, 1971, with the voice of Alastair Sim. This is the only Scrooge movie to win an Oscar (for best short subject animated film, in 1973). The artwork is excellent, capturing perfectly the characters, streets, and interiors of the book, but it is too earnest a film. It is just not much fun.

Scrooge Movies—Computerized

A Christmas Carol, 2009, with Jim Carrey. It is nice that big-budget film versions of *A Christmas Carol* continue to be made, and this adaptation has the benefit of huge acting talent (Jim Carrey, Colin Firth, Bob Hoskins, Gary Oldman, among others). Still, it is unlikely that many will rate this as their favourite film version of Dickens's story. There is little humour or warmth, and it is hard to see the advantage of the 'performance capture' technology—many viewers would prefer to see the real actors performing. Andrea Bocelli's singing of *God Bless Us Every One* over the final credits, however, is a joy.

SCROOGE (1896,
(CHARLES DANA GIBSON)

CHAPTER 6
The Traditional but Surprising Christmas Calendar:

The Twenty Days of Christmas

1. I'm interested to hear what are the Twenty Days of Christmas, but do they really total 20 days? Or are they like the Twelve Days?

—Well they do total 20 calendar days—from dusk on 24th December through the evening of the 13th of January.

CHRISTMAS AT THE MASTHEAD (WM.SMALL C.1879)

2. January 13th ?? And that was really a recognized Christmas Season?

—Yes. Until around the start of the 19th century, everyone appeared to know about the Twenty Days of Christmas, if one can judge by the casual references to them in books and periodicals. In an article in the *Gentlemen's Magazine* of February 1784, for instance, a Mr Beckwith describes Christmas 'near Leedes in Yorkshire' when he was a boy and explains:

'CHRISTMAS IN YORKSHIRE' (DODGSON, *ILN*, 1849)

The festival of Christmas used in this part of the country to hold for *twenty days*, and some persons extended it to Candlemas.

At Gray's Inn in London—one of the Inns of Court (illustrated in chapter 2 above) this regulation on gambling was made in 1629:

> that all playing at dice, cards, or otherwise, in the hall, buttery or butler's chamber, should be thenceforth barred, and forbidden at all times of the year, *the twenty days in Christmas only excepted.*

Chapter 6

The Christmas Calendar —The 20 Days

3. But what's the explanation of the Twenty Days?

GAMBLING, C.1800

—It's an interesting one, but it involves terms that may themselves need explaining: *Octave* and *Epiphany*.

'HERALDING CHRISTMAS' (LUDWIG RICHTER, DRESDEN, 1855)

THE EPIPHANY
—'ADORATION OF THE MAGI'
(*KORBERGER BIBLE*, 1483, GERMANY)

4. O.K.

—The following were the key dates within the twenty days:

- **Christmas Day and its Eve** (beginning at dusk on 24th December);
- **the Octave of Christmas** (which runs for eight days through 1st January—which is also the Feast of the Circumcision);
- **the Epiphany and its Eve** (from the evening of 5th January through 6th January); and
- **the traditional Octave of the Epiphany** (which ran from the evening of 5th January through the day of 13th January).

[Note: The Octave of the Epiphany was 'suppressed' by the Vatican in the late 20th century—to the dismay of many Catholic scholars, who still take issue with the decision. The Anglican Church later followed suit. Again, these church decisions had no effect on civil traditions/laws to which the ancient church calendar had given rise.]

MADONNA OF THE FIR TREE (MARIANNE STOKES, 1925)

5. 'Octave of Christmas' and 'Octave of the Epiphany'—I've never heard of those terms before. I presume 'Octave' has some liturgical meaning?

—Yes. If a holy day has an octave, it means: (a) it is very important, and (b) it is, in effect, celebrated for eight days rather than for just one.

The Mass for each of the seven days following the holy day is treated as if it were the Mass for the holy day itself (even as to vestments, hymns etc. if possible).

III

Chapter 6

The Christmas Calendar —The 20 Days

6. So the Octave of Christmas runs up to New Year's Day?

'BONBON SHOP IN PARIS ON NEW YEAR'S EVE' (*I.L.N.*, 1853)

—Yes, and New Year's Day remains the principal day for giving gifts in France (called *étrennes*) and in some other countries—the legacy of the Roman *Kalends*, and the custom of giving *strenae* on that day. In England, the exchanging of New Year's gifts continued well into the 19th century.

December 26th ('Boxing Day' in the U.K.) was the date for giving presents (of money, usually) to 'social inferiors'— servants, tradesmen etc., who often

LONDON 1860: 'NEW YEAR'S GIFTS IN A TOYSHOP' (*I.L.N.*)

DUC DE BERRY'S HOUSEHOLD GIVING GIFTS (*ÉTRENNES*) AT NEW YEAR (JANUARY PAGE OF *BOOK OF HOURS*, FRANCE, 1410)

Keeping Christmas Well

demanded them as of right; but New Year was the occasion for giving presents to family, friends, and superiors. It is said that the first knitted silk stockings *made* in England (earlier Royal silk stockings had come from Spain) were given as a New Year's present to Queen Elizabeth by her silk-woman in 1561. In New York, too, the giving of New Year's presents continued well into the 19th century.

7. In New York ? Are you sure?

—Yes. For example, the little American book of 1821, *The Children's Friend [>]*, [illustrated in Part I] describes itself as a *'New-Year's Present to the Little Ones from Five to Twelve'* even though, within the book, 'Santeclaus' is said to bring presents on Christmas Eve. The custom of giving gifts at the New Year continued for at least several decades longer. The picture below, for instance, from the *New-York Mirror* in 1841, shows an interestingly dressed gift-giver (with two reindeer) on a New York rooftop, and describes the scene as: *'St. Nicholas, on his New Year's Eve excursion, … in the act of descending a chimney.'*

(*NEW-YORK MIRROR*, 1841)

Chapter 6

The Christmas Calendar —The 20 Days

'NEW YEAR'S GREETINGS' (LUDWIG RICHTER, DRESDEN, 1858)

8. St Nicholas bringing gifts on New Year? Actually, that does seem odd.

—New Year's was an important and sociable holiday in the U.S.—even American presidents held an open house on New Year's Day. Until 1932, anyone could call to the White House (or to the earlier presidential residence in Philadelphia) and shake the president's hand at New Year's. The custom was that anyone waiting in line would be admitted. President Lincoln signed the Emancipation Proclamation on New Year's Day, and his signature is said to look less steady than usual because his right hand was swollen from shaking thousands of hands. This practice continued until 1932.

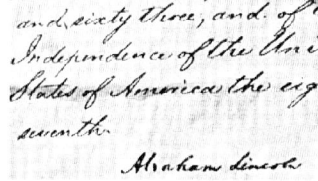

EMANCIPATION PROCLAMATION 1863

9. And they weren't worried about security?

—Apparently not. But in New York, a century

earlier, the mayor's traditional New Year's open house had not worked out quite so well.

10. What happened?

'A NEW YORK POLITICIAN KEEPING OPEN HOUSE ON NEW YEAR'S DAY' (*THE GRAPHIC*, 1871)

—The custom in New York was for New Year to be celebrated in the streets. This was cheerfully tolerated until the late 1820s (the rowdyism and frequent brawls being spoken of, almost affectionately, as 'Tom-and-Jerryism' by the newspapers). In 1827, however, in the term of an elitist

'TOM & JERRY IN A STREET-ROW' (G. & R. CRUIKSHANK, 1821)

mayor, the studied disregard for hierarchy that was central to Christmas street celebrations began to worry the establishment:

> During the celebration greeting the New Year of 1827, however, at least three separate disturbances broke out. Taken together, they forced city officials to reassess their tolerant attitude toward the New Year's frolics. Two were relatively minor affairs. In one riot, the revelers attacked a house in Frankfort Street. In the other, the established lines of social authority were challenged. One group of rioters 'enacted in front of Mr Mayor Hone's house [at

235 Broadway across from City Hall] a scene of disgraceful rage.' ...To abuse his hospitality was not just to offer personal insult, but to flout the emerging middle-class sense of decorum. [From *The road to Mobocracy: Popular Disorder in New York City 1763-1834* by Paul A Gilje, 1987]

Chapter 6

The Christmas Calendar —The 20 Days

BROADWAY, NEW YORK, C. 1809, WITH CITY HALL AT RIGHT (G.HAYWARD)

SANTA CLAUS ON BROADWAY & 34th STREET, NEW YORK, IN 1903

11. Why did opinion change in that year?

Perhaps because society's barriers were shifting. Notably, New York's slaves were emancipated in 1827. Also, Philip Hone, the city's mayor from 1826 to 1827 was very conservative, and there was a hate relationship between him *[right >]* and the immigrant Irish, who very likely were among the New Year's merry-makers.

12. I see.

PHILIP HONE, 1826

—A colourful variation on the French custom of 'calling' on New Year's also existed in New York, with men competing with one another to call on

Keeping Christmas Well

RIGHT:
'ANOTHER YEAR BY THE OLD CLOCK'
[WINSLOW HOMER, HARPER'S BAZAAR, 1870, (BROOKLYN MUSEUM)]

BELOW:
THE NEW YEAR 1869
[WINSLOW HOMER, HARPER'S WEEKLY (BOSTON PUBLIC LIBRARY)]

as many women as possible (and women competing to collect the most calling cards):

Young men in barouches would rattle from one house to another all day long. The ceremony of calling was a burlesque. There was a noisy and hilarious greeting, a glass of wine was swallowed hurriedly, everybody shook hands all round and the callers dashed out and rushed into the carriage and were driven rapidly to the next house. [—Miles]

GENTLEMEN ON THEIR NEW YEAR'S DAY CALLS, (HILL'S MANUAL, U.S., 1873)

An extract from a *New York Times* article of January 3rd, 1888, indicates the tradition must have existed up to a short time before:

A CALLER
(PUNCH, 1890)

— But by far the most noteworthy circumstance in yesterday's history was the almost complete death of the ancient custom of call-making.

ABOVE: BOTTLENECK OF GENTLEMEN CALLERS ON THE STAIRCASE (EDW. & GEO. DALZIEL, 1850)

Chapter 6

The Christmas Calendar —The 20 Days

117

Some of the 'old boys,' however, could be seen yesterday in their spotless kid gloves and shiny

CHILDREN PLAYING AT NEW YEAR CALLING -'ALLOW ME TO PRESENT…'(*HARPER'S YOUNG PEOPLE*, N.Y., 1880)

ties making the rounds as solemnly as they did 30, 40, or 50 years ago… In none of the brownstone districts yesterday were the familiar sights of other New Year's Days to be encountered…

Few carriages were observed bearing the gentlemen about on a pilgrimage of good wishes, and as a matter of fact the ladies themselves did not even deem it necessary to inform their friends that they should not receive. It was taken for granted that they would not. [—*New York Times*, 1888]

'NOT AT HOME' (E. JOHNSON, N.Y., 1873, *BROOKLYN MUSEUM*)

13. Interesting.

—A different, but maybe not unrelated, New Year's calling custom—'First Footing'—still exists in Scotland and in parts of England.

14. What's that?

—It's based on the idea that the first person to call to a house after the start of the New Year determines the luck of the household for the year.

'FIRST FOOTING' (*THE GRAPHIC*, 1884)

15. So what sort of person is considered lucky?

—A tall man with dark hair was usually the preferred choice. He was expected to bring with him small symbolic presents to ensure luck for the household for the year.

16. Why a man?

—Well you may ask. What is certain is that the preference for a man over a woman as the first caller was deep-rooted, and was found even in areas where 'first-footing' was not an important tradition:

'NEW YEAR - FIRST FOOTING' (*I.L.N.*, 1882)

> The idea of the unluckiness of a woman's being the 'first-foot' is extraordinarily widespread; the present writer has met with it in an ordinary London restaurant, where great stress was laid upon a man's opening the place on New Year's morning before the waitresses arrived. [—Miles, 1912]

17. Why with dark hair?

—This is one theory:
It has been suggested by Sir John Rhys that this idea rested in the first instance upon racial antipathy—the natural antagonism of an indigenous dark-haired people to a race of blond invaders. [Miles, 1912]

'GOING FIRST-FOOTING'
(THE GRAPHIC, 1884)

Chapter 6

The Christmas Calendar—The 20 Days

18. What presents were brought?

—Symbols of warmth, food, drink, and wealth. Whisky remains a common present. A 'first-foot presentation pack' (price £4.99) was marketed by one U.K. company for New Year 2000. It contained a piece of coal, a sachet of salt, a coin, and a miniature bottle of Scotch whisky.

'A HAPPY NEW YEAR TO ALL' (K. MEADOWS, *ILLUSTRATED LONDON NEWS*, 1848)

19. O.K. I think I now know quite a lot about the Octave of Christmas but what about the Epiphany and the Octave of the Epiphany (January 6th to January 13th)?

—Well, taking the 'Epiphany' (January 6th) part of it first— this is a very significant feast. It is still a major popular holiday, as well as a religious holy day, in many countries. As we saw, it pre-dated Christmas and for much of history, it was rated a more important holy day than Christmas.

FRENCH BOOK OF HOURS: ADORATION OF THE MAGI (LATE 15th CENTURY)

14. But what does it commemorate?

—As a religious holiday, it commemorates several events, the most important of which in the western Christian church (as opposed to, for instance, the Greek church) is the visit of the Three Wise Men to the stable in Bethlehem. It also commemorates (much more importantly in Greece) the baptism of Christ by John the Baptist (when the voice from heaven said: 'This is My beloved Son in whom I am well pleased') and the miracle at Cana, when Jesus turned water into wine.

FLEMISH BOOK OF HOURS: JOHN THE BAPTIST, C.1440

15. Why the word Epiphany?

—It comes from the Greek word ἐπιφαίνεια *(epiphaineia)* meaning a showing or appearance or manifestation. In the three biblical events described above, something divine was shown or manifested to humans.

Chapter 6

The Christmas Calendar —The 20 Days

'SONG OF THE THREE KINGS' (L.RICHTER, GERMANY, 1869)

16. O.K.

—As a popular holiday (i.e. as a day for celebrations and gifts) it is the most festive day of the Christmas season in much of the world. In Spain and Italy, for instance, it is the day when children are given presents. In Spain, the Three Kings, rather than Santa Claus or Saint Nicholas, are the gift-givers, while in Italy, a witch-like old woman, *La Befana* [from the word *epiphaineia* —Leigh Hunt, 1835], is the present-giver.

'BEFANA IN CASA' ITALY (B.PINELLI, 1800S) >

17. I know a lot of people in the US and in England who have never heard of the Epiphany.

—Yes, and that is very surprising.

Keeping Christmas Well

18. Why?

—Because the Epiphany or Twelfth Day (with its Eve, Twelfth Night) remained—until the second half of the 19th century—'the most popular day throughout the Christmas' in England [—Sandys, 1852]. In parts of the U.S., also, it was regarded as the best day for Christmas entertainments. It was the big party day of Christmas.

TWELFTH NIGHT.
(*ABOVE:* ISSAC CRUIKSHANK, LONDON, 1794)

19. Where in the U.S.?

—In Virginia, for instance (where George and Martha Washington chose to be married *[right]* on the morning of 6th January—Twelfth Day):

(J. B. STEARNS, C.1853)

In Virginia, Twelfth Night was the focus of the secular Christmas season. The most sumptuous balls, with many guests and lasting several days, were mounted at the finest homes. The college, the Indian school, and the grammar school, shut since December 16, only reopened

CHRISTMAS BALL, MOUNT VERNON, 1798 (J.L.G. FERRIS)

after Twelfth Day. Plantation classrooms were suddenly unbarred as well. Dancing, drinking, eating, and games ruled. [—M. Olmert, *Colonial Williamsburg Journal*, 2004.]

20. And in England?

—The following descriptions of Epiphany celebrations in England from the 16th, 17th, 18th, 19th and 20th centuries give an idea of how festive the holiday was (and also how entrenched it was in the national psyche (even after Puritan times)—and how surprising and sudden its end:

EPIPHANY/TWELFTH NIGHT PARTY WITH 'TWELFTH CAKE,' ENGLAND, C.1800 [IMAGE: AUSTENONLY.COM]

1508 AD:

On the Epiphany, 1508, the Duke of Buckingham had 459 to dinner,—

> of different degrees, including 134 gentry, with two minstrels, six trumpets, four waits [musicians], and four players. [—Sandys]

The food menu, which included swans and peacocks, is too long to list, but the quantity of ale provided (in addition to wines) in instructive: for the Epiphany, 200 gallons of ale had been laid on; for the less important Christmas Day entertainment, by comparison, a mere 171 gallons of ale had been provided.

'TWELFTH NIGHT KING' (R. SEYMOUR, 1836)

Chapter 6

The Christmas Calendar —The 20 Days

1623 AD:
On this night [6th January] much masking in the Strand, Cheapside, Holburne or Fleet-street ... [—Ellis]

'TWELFTH NIGHT - THE KING DRINKS!' (J. JORDAENS, C.1640)

1668 AD:
Samuel Pepys recorded that he served his Twelfth Night guests 'an excellent cake which cost me near 20 s[hillings]... which was cut into twenty pieces, there being... so many of our company... And so to dancing again, and singing, ... till about two in the morning.'

'TWELFTH NIGHT CHARACTERS' WITH TWELFTH CAKE IN FOREGROUND
(ROBT. CRUIKSHANK, 1836)

1725 AD:
The Twelfth Day itself is one of the greatest of the Twelve, and of more jovial Observation

than the others for the visiting of Friends and Christmas-Gambols. [—Bourne]

1809 AD:
...none of the characters knew one another... we had such frightful masks that it was enough to kill one with laughing at putting them on... [—Jane Austen's niece, Fanny Knight, describes her family's Twelfth Night party.]

'TWELFTH NIGHT PARTY' (GEO. CRUIKSHANK, *COMIC ALMANAC*, 1844)

1835 AD:
Then followed drawing for king and queen... Then games of all the received kinds... our characters imitated a court... Then came supper... the good humour, the wine, the wit, the poetry... fused all hearts together... till breakfast (*6 o'clock in the morning*). [Leigh-Hunt]

1843 AD:
...Heaped up on the floor, ... immense twelfth-cakes... [—Dickens, *A Christmas Carol*]

'A TWELFTH NIGHT JUVENILE BALL' (*I.L.N.*, 1852)

Chapter 6

The Christmas Calendar —The 20 Days

Keeping Christmas Well

1852 AD:
Some of the most splendid entertainments were given on this day; and in our times it is *probably the most popular day throughout the Christmas*, thanks to the Twelfth Cake and Drawing for Characters, with other amusements. [—Sandys]

'CUTTING TWELFTH CAKE' (J. SAYERS, POLITICAL CARTOON, 1798)

1860 AD:
As the fashion of Twelfth cakes declined, the pastry cooks had to push their sale in every way possible, not being very particular as to overstepping the law, by getting rid of them by means of drawings, raffles and lotteries… and M. Louis Dethier was summoned at Bow Street on 26th December 1860, for keeping an office… for the purpose of carrying on a lottery 'under the name, device, and pretence of a distribution of Twelfth cakes.' [—Ashton]

TWELFTH NIGHT CHARACTER CARDS LABEL, SHOWING VAUXHALL GARDENS, LONDON, WITH LARGE TWELFTH CAKE AND 'THE MASTER OF CEREMONIES INTRODUCING HIS FRIENDS ON TWELFTH NIGHT' (A. PARK, C.1834)

1894 AD:
The custom of having a Twelfth Cake and electing a King and Queen has now died out,

and is only known by tradition; so utterly died out indeed, that in the British Library there is not a single sheet of Twelfth-night Characters to show the younger race of students what they were like. [—Ashton]

INSPECTING A TWELFTH NIGHT CHARACTER CARD (R.SEYMOUR 1836)

1912 AD:
Though the Epiphany has ceased to be a popular festival in England, it was once a very high day indeed. [—Miles]

From the above, it seems that the English Epiphany celebrations—much loved for more than half a millennium—disappeared without trace between 1852 and 1894. This did not happen because of war or coercion, and nothing like it happened anywhere else.

21. What about the US? Didn't it happen there too?

—Yes, but in America, it had been more a locally celebrated holiday than a great national holiday. If Thanksgiving suddenly ceased to be celebrated in America, and forty years from now, no one remembered exactly how it had been celebrated, and why it had stopped being celebrated, that would be similar in significance to the disappearance of the Epiphany in England, particularly when it continued to be celebrated in other European countries.

'GIVING TWELFTH-CAKE TO THE POOR,' FRANCE (*LAROUSSE GASTRONOMIQUE*) >

22. So what happened? If the Twelfth Day and

its Eve used to be so popular, why are they not celebrated now in the U.S. and in England?

—Powerful forces conspired against the poor old Twelfth Day. Ultimately, the Industrial Revolution and Capitalism killed it off, but the groundwork for its elimination in those countries had been laid earlier. In Ireland, by contrast, which remained an agricultural society until recently, the celebration of Epiphany (*'Little Christmas'*) prospered well into the twentieth century, certainly in rural Cork. The day was marked with a family party and an old-fashioned spread of cakes and desserts (very much in the style of those shown *right* >) on the night of January 6th.

DESSERT SPREAD (*MRS BEETON*, 1891 ED)

23. I thought it was called 'Women's Christmas' (*Nollaig na mBan*) in Ireland?

—That's another name for it. The theory is that women need do no work on that day (the next day—St Distaff's day—having marked their post-Christmas return to the traditional women's job of spinning). The observance of *Nollaig na mBan* has survived (in Cork, at least) and a tradition now is for groups of women to go to restaurants on that day—often booking every table.

'YOUNG HUSBAND FIRST MARKETING'
(LILLY MARTIN SPENCER, 1880)

'STUDIO LUNCH'
(H. S. MOBRAY, *C*.1880)

24. The quotations about English Epiphany celebrations refer to a 'Twelfth Cake.' I don't mean to get distracted by a petty detail, but I've never heard of a Twelfth Cake, and it seems to have been of central significance. What is a Twelfth Cake anyway, and why would a cake make January 6th 'the most popular day of Christmas'?

Chapter 6

The Christmas Calendar —The 20 Days

—The Twelfth Cake is not a petty detail. It was one of the important festive institutions of the year—more significant, really, than the Christmas turkey or goose.

QUEEN VICTORIA'S TWELFTH CAKE OF 1849 (ABOUT 30 INCHES IN DIAMETER)

25. What do you mean?

—The principal significance of the Twelfth Cake was as the centre of the night's entertainment in which everyone acted a character part.

26. Could you explain that?

'THE KING DRINKS - 12th NIGHT IN FRANCE' (*I.L.N.*, 1852)

—Traditionally, a bean (or a coin) was concealed in the cake and whoever got the bean or the coin became 'King.' Other accounts, including that of Andrew Herrick, describe a bean and a pea in

TWELFTH NIGHT GUESTS STUDY THE CHARACTERS ASSIGNED TO THEM
(GEO. CRUIKSHANK, LONDON, 1807)

the cake, with the recipient of the pea becoming 'Queen.' The characters to be played could also be determined in other ways—for instance, by a card drawn from a special Twelfth Night set, or by an item that had been baked into each piece of cake, or else assigned to them by the 'King.' '...the characters were to be supported throughout the night' [—Sandys, 1852]

TWELFTH NIGHT (R. SEYMOUR, 1836) WITH INSPECTION OF CHARACTER CARDS AND THE SERVING OF TWELFTH CAKE *(LEFT)* AND WASSAIL BOWL *(RIGHT)*

27. What sort of roles did they play?

—They seemed to vary over time. In 1676, this account of a jolly party on an English warship (held during the day of 6th January) was written by the ship's chaplain, the Rev. Henry Teonge:

... we had much myrth on board, for wee had a great kake made, in which was put a beane for the king, a pease for the queen, a cloave for the knave, a forked stick for the cuckold, a ragg for the slut. The kake was cut into severall pieces in the great cabin, and all put into a napkin, out of which every one took his piece, as out of a lottery; then each piece is broaken to see what was in it, which caused much laughter, to see our leiuetenant prove the cuckold, and more to see us tumble one over the other in the cabin, by reason of the ruff weather.

TEONGE'S TWELFTH NIGHT AT SEA, 1676

Chapter 6

The Christmas Calendar —The 20 Days

In the 18th century (and also in Leigh-Hunt's 1835 party) typical characters were 'ministers, maids-of-honour, and other attendants of a court' [—Sandys, 1852].

28. And 19th century Twelfth Night cards?

—They usually had a character sketch and a verse.

< LORD GOLDLACE
GREAT BRITAIN HER GLORY MAY OWE TO THE SAILOR;
BUT, FOR MINE, I'M INDEBTED ALONE TO MY TAILOR;
FOR MEN OF MY PEDIGREE HELD IT NO SIN TO BE GLITTERING WITHOUT ALTHOUGH EMPTY WITHIN.

[BY R. DOYLE, ILLUSTRATED LONDON NEWS, 1848]

MISS CAROLINE COQUETTE >
I'M A FLIRT—I AVOW IT—THERE'S NO ONE OCCASION
ON WHICH I DON'T GET UP A BIT OF FLIRTATION;
NOW IT'S FRED, NOW IT'S HARRY, WHO THINKS ME HIS OWN,
THEN STANDS STARING AGHAST WHEN HE FINDS THE BIRD FLOWN!

Keeping Christmas Well

< FARMER MANGLEWURZEL
I'SE A ROUGH HONEST FARMER LOIKE—CES,
   SO I BE, ZUR;
AND MY TALK'S OF GUANO AND WHEAT DO
   YOU SEE, ZUR?
MY WITS MAY BE DULL, AND MY BARK MAY
   BE ROUGH,
BUT AT HEART, I'LL GO BOUND, I'SE A GOOD
   BIT OF STUFF.

[BY R. DOYLE, *ILLUSTRATED LONDON NEWS*, 1848]

TWELFTH NIGHT KING >
THE MAXIM'S RIFE IN LAW-BOOKS DREAR
   AND LONG,
WHATEVER HAP—THE KING CAN DO NO
   WRONG.
SO NOW, TO-NIGHT, WHATE'ER MY DEEDS
   MAY BE,
REMEMBER—NO ONE'S TO FIND FAULT
   WITH ME.

29. What was the Twelfth Cake like to eat?

—It varied. There was no consistent recipe (or consistent size—some of them were huge). Robert Herrick referred to a plum cake (apparently unfrosted). Martha Washington's interesting recipe *[at top >]* begins: 'Take 40 eggs…'

TWELFTH CAKE
[MOUNT VERNON, VA.]
AMERICA

Twelfth Cakes remain important in many countries: e.g. *galettes des Rois [middle >]* in France (with different regional recipes), and the *roscon* in Spain *[below >]* (cream-filled, with a King-figure and bean, and supplied with a gold cardboard crown). There was widespread consensus in England that the *taste* of a Twelfth Cake was the least important aspect of it (but other countries may have had different priorities).

'GALETTE DES ROIS'
[LAROUSSE GASTRONQ.]
FRANCE

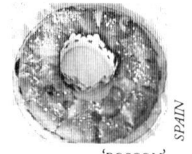

'ROSCON'
SPAIN

30. I see.

ENGLISH TWELFTH CAKE, (GEFFRYE MUSEUM, LONDON)

—The English cake, however, grew to *look* very dramatic. This account of the traffic-stopping appeal to children of the mere sight of an English Twelfth Cake) was written in 1852:

> The French Twelfth-cake is still plain in appearance, containing a bean; it was composed, about 250 years since, of flour, honey, ginger and pepper; they are, however, far exceeded in appearance by the rich, frosted, almond-pasted, festooned, bedizened, and carefully-ornamented cakes of the English pattern, gladdening the eyes of joyful, holiday young people, and through them the hearts of their parents. The eager groupings of passers-by, to see the shop-windows crowded with these elegant productions of confectionary science, causes stoppages in our highways and thoroughfares, with reiterated 'Move-ons' from our policemen. About twenty-five years ago there was one exhibited, said to weigh one ton... Speaking from memory, and with a taste somewhat blunted to these enjoyments, the flavour was somewhat below the average... [—Sandys, 1852]

Chapter 6

The Christmas Calendar —The 20 Days

'TWELFTH NIGHT IN LONDON STREETS' (*DRAWN:* R.SEYMOUR, 1836). THOSE WHO PAUSED TO LOOK AT THE PASTRYCOOKS' TWELFTH-CAKE DISPLAYS RISKED HAVING THEIR CLOTHES PINNED TO ANOTHER'S (OR NAILED TO THE SHOP-FRONT) BY STREET URCHINS, 'ELVES OF THE PAVE' [—LEIGH-HUNT, 1835]. DESCRIBING THE MISSPENT DAY OF ONE SUCH 'ELF,' LEIGH-HUNT SUMMED UP: 'HIS MOTHER THINKS HERSELF LUCKY IF HE IS NOT TRANSPORTED.'

31. But I am still surprised that anyone considered January 13th an important Day of Christmas.

—Well, have you ever heard of St Knut's Day?

32. No.

'KIRSTI'S SLEIGH RIDE' (C. LARSSON, SWEDEN, 1901)

—That's a name for the 13th January (the twentieth day of Christmas) in Sweden (and Finland and Norway), and it's traditional in those countries for Christmas decorations to be left up until St Knut's Day.

33. Who is Saint Knut?

—He had other names as well: Canutus and Canute II. He became the first Danish King of England in 1017 (where he is remembered for an attempt—unsuccessful—to order back the tide.) He was also King of Denmark, and for a time had power in Norway and part of Sweden. He was a Viking who had a soft spot for Christmas.

34. But why was January 13th named after him?

CHRISTMAS BANQUET IN SWEDEN (C. LARSSON, 1904)

—At a time when the church required people to fast on certain days, he made it law that no one was required to fast between Christmas and January 13th—the Octave of the Epiphany. The 18th century quote at the end of Chapter 4 which refers to the 12 (or 13) and 20 days of Christmas, finishes with an interesting reference to the 'Laws

of Canutus' (made in the 11th century):
> For in the Laws of Canutus, it is ordered that no man shall fast from Christmas Day till after the Octave of the Epiphany, except he do it out of Choice, or it be commanded him of the Priest. [—Bourne]

35. So Christmas in Sweden, Norway and Finland lasts until January 13th?

—Yes, but in that region of long winter nights, it seems that many people dislike ending their Christmas even then. Traditionally the edible decorations are given to the children to eat on that day.

CHRISTMAS TREE, SWEDEN
(CARL LARSSON, 1907)

36. In that context, the U.S. Christmas seems very short. Some Americans think Christmas is over at the end of 25th December —before the Twelve Days of Christmas have even started (and when there are 39 more days of Christmas in Mexico and 19 more days of Christmas in Sweden). Other Americans think it's over by the end of New Year's Day. It's hard to think anyone in the U.S. ever celebrated Christmas until February.

—Very true.

'CHRISTMAS COMES BUT ONCE A YEAR'
(T. NAST, 1881
HARPER'S WEEKLY,
NEW YORK)

Keeping Christmas Well

37. Now, about that business of the night being the start of the day at Christmas, and the Days of Christmas not all being of equal length?

—An interesting subject, and it brings us to one of the more contentious aspects of Christmas— historical religious opposition to it.

38. O.K.

—But first another interlude chapter.

A TWELFTH-CAKE DELIVERY, LONDON, C. 1800

CHAPTER 7

—*Interlude*—
Movies at Christmas

NEW YORK CITY HOTEL AT CHRISTMAS, WITH DOG, WREATH, TREE, & DRINK
(*THE THIN MAN*)

A short, personal list (continued in chapter 10) of movies that add something to Christmas. Some are well-known, but you may not have thought of them before as 'Christmas movies.' Others are forgotten, and a couple, you may never have heard of at all. Many of them are old black-and-white films, and a few of them, frustratingly, are not available on DVD (or VHS) at time of writing.

The Apartment

Eyebrows have been raised at our first choice—*The Apartment*, 1960 (Director: Billy Wilder).

Set in the amoral world of serial philanderers in a New York insurance company, it seems not quite to fit into the box marked 'Christmas movie.' Yet *The Apartment* is *the* Christmas movie for grown-ups—capturing better than any other the Christmas extremes of loneliness and cosiness.

It is set between Halloween and New Year, and in the street scenes, you can almost feel the bite of a cold New York winter. This film has the best (by miles) Christmas office party, the best Christmas bar (on Christmas Eve, with juke box and drunks who have nowhere to go,

including an off-duty Santa)—'Don't you know what night this is?' the barman asks. 'I know, Charley, I know, I work for the outfit,' Santa replies before sadly picking up his beard from the counter and leaving.

It has the best Chinese restaurant, the cosiest apartment-sized Christmas tree on a table: 'snugsville' indeed, as one of the movie's characters accurately describes the atmosphere it creates. The two principal characters, C.C. Baxter (Jack Lemmon) and Fran (Shirley MacLaine), never kiss or hug and hardly touch: Fran tries

to kill herself on Christmas Eve night, and is barely conscious for Christmas Day. Yet no other movie has ever created a more powerful sense of intimacy between two people, or leaves you feeling better about life.

Two good people in a bad world saved by love and by Christmas—

what more could you want from a Christmas movie?

The Thin Man

Chapter 7

Interlude

Movies at Christmas

The Thin Man, 1934 (Director: W. S. Van Dyke). Never listed as a Christmas movie, *The Thin Man* captures par excellence the exuberant pagan traditions of Christmas (being enjoyed as if the Puritans never made anyone feel guilty about them). The movie has neither children nor churches, but almost drowns (unashamedly) in drink. Nora (Myrna Loy) spends much of Christmas Eve with an ice pack on her head. [After joining Nick (William Powell) in a bar earlier, and on hearing that he already had six martinis, she had directed the waiter to line up as many in front of her.] Later that day in their New York hotel, they host a party attended by old friends of Nick (ex-cons among them).

Reporters arrive and ask Nora if Nick is working on

Keeping Christmas Well

a case. 'Yes. A case of Scotch,' she replies *[<]*.

Trays of drinks ('ammunition') are passed, the crowd drunkenly sings 'O Christmas Tree...' Nick gets a present of a pellet gun *[>]*, with which he shoots the Christmas-tree balloons. Their fox terrier, Asta, gets his own fire hydrant *[below]*.

Not a standard 'Christmas movie,' just fun.

THE THIN MAN, 1934

MIRACLE ON 34TH STREET

Chapter 7

Interlude

Movies at Christmas

Miracle on 34th Street, 1947 (Dir.: George Seaton). This movie is so good it made a Christmas icon out of a New York department store. It's on every list of Christmas movies, and there's not much new to say about it, but it's so brilliant, that we had to include it. It's smart, never mawkish (Natalie Wood is more child than actress, Maureen O'Hara is formidable, and Edmund Gwenn obviously *is* Santa Claus), and it builds to a wonderfully peculiar, but really good miracle. Visually, it's fascinating—scenes were filmed on the streets of 1940s New York and inside Macy's.

As with so many Christmas movies (note the setting of the two movies above) New York City is one of the principal stars—some achievement for a town that re-opens for business on the First of the Twelve Days of Christmas.

Bachelor Mother, 1939 (Director: Garson Kanin).

This is another film that is never listed as a Christmas move, but it's hard to know why not. Polly (Ginger Rogers) loses her job in a New York department store (where else?) on Christmas Eve; also on Christmas Eve, a baby described as 'wonderful' (identity unknown, but with a destiny for changing lives) is abandoned in a doorway; a wonderfully crazy Donald Duck toy begins and ends the film; Ginger is Cinderella-ed on New Year's Eve by the millionaire David (David Niven); and Ginger even dances.

A very smart movie. The scenes in which people determinedly believe what they want to believe—David's blind faith in an insane instruction from a medical book (it turns out the pages were stuck together), his father's belief that the foundling baby must his grandson—are as perceptive about human weakness as they are funny.

THE BISHOP'S WIFE

Chapter 7

Interlude

Movies at Christmas

The Bishop's Wife, 1947 (Director: Henry Coster). The only movie on this list (with the possible exception of *It's a Wonderful Life*) inspired by the religious side of Christmas. The angel Dudley (Cary Grant) appears in answer to the prayers of Bishop Henry Brougham (David Niven) who soon wishes the handsome angel would go back where he came from after it becomes clear that he fancies the bishop's wife, Julia (Loretta Young). David Niven's performance is particularly funny (and he is given some of the best scenes, as when he is miraculously

glued to a chair). A likeable, intelligent film—uncompromisingly 'a Christmas movie.'

HOLIDAY INN

Holiday Inn, 1942 (Director: Mark Sandrich).

Perhaps best known as the movie in which the song 'White Christmas' was first aired, this is so much better than the leaden

White Christmas movie made twelve years later. Fred Astaire is at his sparkling best, Bing's voice in 1942 was at the top of its form, and the plot

races along. Aficionados of evolving Christmas design should keep an eye out in the urban nightclub/dressing room scenes for the synthetic Christmas trees, which were all the rage in the 1940s.

Chapter 7

Interlude

Movies at Christmas

Holiday Affair, 1949 (Director: Don Hartman).

—Fascinating for the time, the place, the setting, and the casting—Robert Mitchum in a Christmas movie??? One of the surprisingly few movies of the period about a woman widowed by World War II (Connie, played by Janet Leigh) and how she manages (with difficulty).

Connie supports a young son, and her job as a 'comparison shopper' takes her through New York department stores. There's nothing fake about the film—Connie (not very good at her job) is exhausted at the end of the working day. She has a suitor—the decent but unexciting Carl played by Wendell Corey (an expert in such roles) but she is still in love with her dead husband.

Then Steve (Robert Mitchum) appears, selling toys in a department store. A veteran, he saves Connie from losing her job when he hears she is a war widow, but then he is fired. As unpredictable as Carl is reliable, he is saving to go to California to become a boat designer, but then spends his savings on an expensive toy train for Connie's son.

As with so many Christmas movies, it makes good use of New York settings (including Central Park Zoo). A feel-good movie ultimately, but particularly interesting as a post-World-War-II movie in which the war is still having an effect.

BARMAN— 'DON'T YOU KNOW WHAT NIGHT THIS IS?'
SANTA— 'I KNOW, CHARLEY, I KNOW, I WORK FOR THE OUTFIT.'
(*THE APARTMENT*, 1960)

CHAPTER 8

THE VIGILS OF CHRISTMAS

1. So what's this business about the days of Christmas not being all of the same length?

CHRISTMAS EVE (C. GRAHAM, *H.W.*) 1888,

—It's because the origin of Christmas was a church holiday. As we already saw, not all days are equal in the eyes of the Christian church. Sundays and feast days rank higher than other days, and feast days are by no means all equal to one another.

2. O.K.

—A feast day might, for instance, have been classed (until the second half of the 20th century, when a more prosaic terminology was introduced) a 'Double of the First Class,' a 'Double of the Second Class,' a 'Double Major,' a 'Double Minor,' a 'Semi-double,' or a mere 'Simple.'

3. Great names, but what do they mean?

—The rank of a feast day, in effect, determines its liturgical length.

CHRISTMAS EVE (*CHRISTMAS IN ART & SONG*, 1879)

4. What on earth does that mean?

—Remember those other great names—the names

for the Canonical Hours (the prescribed devotions performed at fixed times of the day)—Matins (during the night), Lauds (sunrise), Prime (first hour of day), Terce (third hour of day), Sext (sixth hour of day, or midday), None (ninth hour of day), Vespers (before sunset), and Compline (before retiring)?

5. Um …

—Well, until relatively modern times, almost everyone in the western Christian world was familiar with those exotic terms. In fact, for many centuries, the canonical hours were so much part of the popular culture that the bells summoning the monks for the performance of them served as the people's clock.

'CHURCH BELLS' (R. SEYMOUR, *BOOK OF CHRISTMAS*, 1836)

6. O.K.

—It was also common knowledge that not all feast days were the same length—that a higher-ranking feast might commence at Vespers (First Vespers) on the vigil, and continue through Vespers (Second Vespers) and Compline on the following day. So, liturgically speaking, a higher-ranking feast day lasted for more than 24 hours, and a lower-ranking feast day might be shorter than 24 hours.

'VESPERS BELL—CALL TO EVENING PRAYER' (L. RICHTER, GERMANY, 1842)

7. So, a really important feast day…?

Chapter 8

The Vigils of Christmas

—Well, we already saw that the very important feast of Christmas (and, before Vatican II, the feast of the Epiphany) was celebrated for eight days—an Octave.

BOOK OF HOURS NATIVITY PAGE, FRANCE C. 1460 [GLASGOW UNIVERSITY]

8. That seems incredibly complicated, but you say that in the past, ordinary people knew all that stuff?

—Yes, and ordinary people loved vigils—loved them too much, in the opinion of people in power.

9. What do you mean?

SNOWBALLING ON CHRISTMAS EVE (DODGSON, *I.L.N.*, 1853)

—Well, here is a definition of 'vigil' from the text *Learning the Breviary*, 1932, by Bernard A. Hausmann S.J. :

> VIGIL: a day of penitential character observed as a preparation for the greater feast.

Keeping Christmas Well

10. O.K.

—And here are scenes of how people in fact observed the vigils. These are two paintings of Twelfth Night entertainments— the Vigil of the Epiphany; (and following are two engravings of the Vigil of Christmas).

ABOVE C.1634

DETAILS FROM TWO PAINTINGS OF TWELFTH NIGHT CELEBRATIONS (BOTH BY DAVID TENIERS, FLANDERS)

< LEFT C.1635

'VIGIL OF CHRISTMAS—CHRISTMAS EVE' (G.CRUIKSHANK, 1838 *ABOVE*, 1837 *BELOW*)

11. I see.

—Ultimately the subject of vigils—in effect the commencement on the previous day of certain holy days or solemnities—became a very contentious issue.

12. Why?

—Vigils often became part of the civil law—a law much appreciated by workers (and resented by employers etc.) as it meant the working day ended early on Saturday, at the hour that was deemed to be the start of Sunday. Here is an example of an English law:

CHURCH BELLS (VIZETELLY, *CHRISTMAS WITH THE POETS*, 1851)

> For in the year 958, when King Edgar made his Ecclesiastical Laws, we find one made to this very purpose: in which it is ordered that the Sabbath or Sunday shall be observed from Saturday at noon till the light appear on Monday morning. [—Bourne, 1725.]

13. From noon?

—Yes, but 'noon,' in fact, was three in the afternoon— *hora nona* (the 'ninth hour' according the old Roman method of timekeeping which the church followed).

That the Noon-Tide signifies Three in the Afternoon, according to our present

MONASTIC SUNDIAL (WITH *HORA NONA* AT MID-LEFT) KILMALKEDAR, CO KERRY, IRELAND, 7th CENTURY AD

Chapter 8

The Vigils of Christmas

accounts; and this practice, I conceive, continued down to the Reformation. Three in the Afternoon was *Hora Nona* in the Latin account, and therefore called Noon. [—Bourne, 1725]

14. So why do we call midday 'noon'?

—Blame hungry monks. Fasting monks were allowed to eat only after the 3.00 pm recitation

'THOUGHTS OF CHRISTMAS' (*EVERY SATURDAY JOURNAL*, 1871)

of *None*—the fixed set of devotions (or 'Office') to be said at that hour. Not surprisingly, pressure grew for the recitation of *None* to drift earlier in the day (closer to midday), which happened.
—Hence our word 'noon.'

MONKS WITH FOOD & DRINK (WALLPAPER DESIGN, WM CAMPBELL WALLPAPER CO. C.1912)

I wish they had never been guilty of a worse fraud than this. [—Bourne, 1725]

15. Three in the afternoon is still early.

—Too early, the killjoys would decide. As a result of how people made use of this free time (i.e. instead of

FROM '*LI LIVRES DOU SANTÉ*' (FRANCE, 13th CENTURY)

Chapter 8

The Vigils of Christmas

fasting, they enjoyed themselves) the start of Sunday vigil was delayed by a few hours, moved from three o'clock to Saturday evening:

CHRISTMAS STORYTELLING (*I.L.N.* 19th CENT.)

> It is, that in the year 1332, at a Provincial Council held by Archbishop Mepham at Magfield, after complaint made, that instead of fasting upon the Vigils, they ran out to all the excesses of Riot, &c, it was appointed 'that the Solemnity for Sunday should begin upon Saturday in the evening, and not before...'
> [—John Brand, Bourne-Brand.]

(J. TENNIEL, 1864)

16. So...

—There's more. The Catholic Church had a great many Holy Days, and these were a particular

CHRISTMAS EVE (DODGSON, *I.L.N.*, 1848)

source of annoyance to stern Protestant reformers, not least because each Holy Day was preceded by its vigil, which meant fewer hours worked and more incentive for 'licentiousness.' One of those who disapproved of the numerous Holy Days and their vigils was the very-stern-indeed English clergyman and antiquarian, John Brand. 'Industry will be no bad preparation to the Sabbath,' he wrote in 1776, advocating that workers should continue with their labour during the vigil of the Holy Day.

VIGIL OF THE EPIPHANY (J. JORDAENS, ANTWERP, C. 1640)

'Considered in a political view,' opined Brand, 'much harm has been done by that prodigal Waste of Days very falsely called Holy Days in the Church of Rome. They have greatly favoured the cause of Vice and Dissipation without doing any essential service to that of rational Religion. Complaints seem to have been made in almost every Synod and Council of the Licentiousness introduced by the keeping of Vigils.' [—Bourne-Brand.]

VIGIL OF THE EPIPHANY: WASSAILING FRUIT TREES IN DEVON (VIZETELLY, 1851)

VIGIL—TWELFTH NIGHT MERRYMAKING IN FARMER SHAKESHAFT'S BARN (PHIZ, C. 1840)

155

Chapter 8

The
Vigils
of
Christmas

THE VIGIL OF
CHRISTMAS

ABOVE:
'CHRISTMAS EVE'
['JULNATT'] (ALF
WALLANDER,
SWEDEN, 1895)

RIGHT:
FROM 'THE DAY
BEFORE CHRISTMAS'
(CARL LARSSON,
SWEDEN, 1892)

BELOW:
NATIVITY WITH
TIRED MADONNA
AND NOVICE ANGELS,
1893 (MARIANNE
PREINDELSBERGER
STOKES, AUSTRIA &
ENGLAND 1855-1927)

Keeping Christmas Well

'CHRISTMAS EVE – GOING TO MASS' (L. ARNOLD, 1888, GERMANY)

CHAPTER 9

The Banning of Christmas

1. O.K. So I'm beginning to see how the killjoys' annoyance at vigils, and the banning of Christmas by Puritans etc., might be connected. Was England the first place that Christmas was banned?

'BRINGING THE YULE LOG' (E.&G. DALZIEL, *CHRISTMAS COMES BUT ONCE A YEAR*, 1850)

—No. Geneva in Switzerland was probably the first.

2. Why Geneva?

—At the beginning of the 16th century, it was the centre of the religious ideology that would later be called Calvinism. It had taken a firm hold in the city even before Jean (John) Calvin (a French lawyer, who would rule Geneva with an iron glove) settled there in the 1530s. Not everyone agreed with Calvin's views (including his extreme hostility to the celebration of Christmas) and he was exiled from the city between 1538 and 1541. After his return, the Genevan Council formally

VIEW TOWARDS GENEVA (J-A LINCK C.1800)

CALVIN LEAVING GENEVA IN 1538 (VAN MUYDEN, 1909)

banned Christmas in 1550, but the ban was not a success; it provoked (as it would later do in England) intense resistance, some of it apparently violent.

3. What was the Calvinists' problem with Christmas anyway?

—They had so many, it is hard to list them all.

4. Well, give me a summary.

JOHN CALVIN (SCHEFFER 1858)

—Calvinists (which we can use as shorthand for all the religious groups that shared Calvin's beliefs, such as Puritans and Presbyterians) believe solely in the authority of the Bible. They considered that Christmas was not authorized by Scriptures and was an invention of the pre-Reformation Catholic Church, and a relatively late (i.e. fourth century) invention of that church. Christians of the first and second centuries had *not* celebrated the birth of Christ.

5. Go on.

—The Puritans and Calvinists believed that only one day a week—Sunday—should be kept as a holy day, that this was what the Bible directed (although the point is sometimes made that Jesus himself, and the first Christians, had kept Saturday as their Sabbath).

CHURCH OF THE NATIVITY, BETHLEHEM, FIRST DEVELOPED IN 4th CENTURY AD BY HELENA, MOTHER OF THE EMPEROR CONSTANTINE (ENGR. LEMAITRE, 1845)

They believed that no other holy day should be observed, and no saint's day should be observed;

HELENA, MOTHER OF CONSTANTINE

and of all the holy days established by the pre-Reformation Catholic church, they thought Christmas was the most objectionable.

6. Why? Would they not want to celebrate the date of Christ's birth?

—Well, it seems that there is no historical record of the actual date of Christ's birth; and in the absence of a reliable historical record, every month of the year has been suggested as a possibility at one time or another.

NATIVITY (W. SKOCZYLAS, POLAND, 1931) >

7. O.K.

—But even if the date were known, they did not believe that the date of his physical birth should be observed. The Bible did not take account of birthdays. The day a Christian martyr died might be remembered, but not the day of his birth.

8. I see.

—Also, the particular date of 25th December was a huge problem to them.

9. Again, why?

—Because although there was no biblical or Chris-

AFTER THE CHRISTMAS MORNING SERVICE AT THE AMERICAN CATHEDRAL IN PARIS (J. BÉRAUD, 1890)

tian tradition of celebrating birthdays, there was a *pagan* tradition of celebrating birthdays. December 25th was the Roman date of the winter solstice. Before it was made a Christian holiday in

Chapter 9

The Banning of Christmas

Rome, it was an important pagan holiday there—*Natalis Invicti*, the Birthday of the Unconquered [Sun] *(Sol Invictus)*.

10. Huh?

SOL INVICTUS IN MITHRAEUM UNDER CIRCUS MAXIMUS, ROME (3rd CENT. AD)

—Well, sun worship was important in Rome. In relation to the history of Christianity, it is probably most significant that December 25th was celebrated as the birthday of one particular sun god, Mithras.

11. Mithras? I've never heard of a Roman god named Mithras.

CHRISTMAS MORNING (E.F.BREWTNALL, 1846-1902)

—In fact, he was a god of Asian origin. It is speculated that his cult was brought to Rome by soldiers. It was an extremely influential cult in Rome in the early centuries of Christianity.

12. What sort of cult was it?

—Many people think its most interesting feature was that it had a lot in common with Christianity—his followers believed in an eternal afterlife of the soul, for instance. Mithras was believed to have been born on earth miraculously (usually said to have sprung from a stone). Traditional explanations say that Mithras killed the divine bull, from whose body sprang the parts of nature beneficial to man. He was then taken up to heaven, where he would watch over the faithful until his second coming. In recent decades, however, there has been little consensus about any aspect of Mithraism.

MITHRAS (BRITISH MUSEUM)

13. O.K.

His cult was apparently men-only, but otherwise it conducted itself well, and was known for demanding a high standard of behaviour from its followers. Many, if not most, Roman soldiers belonged to it, and it was more or less the official military religion.

14. So does that mean that the choice of 25th December as the date for celebrating Christ's birth was just a tactical move by the Christian church—because it was the date of Mithras's birthday?

CHRISTMAS MORNING (F.C.HASSAM, 1892)

Chapter 9

The Banning of Christmas

—It might have been, but there was nothing unusual about that. That was pretty well the policy of the Christian church. If there was a pagan custom it believed it could not eradicate, it tended to convert it into a Christian custom.

15. Like all those wells and trees you see in Ireland that were sacred to the pagans and now are sacred to a saint?

ST DECLAN'S HOLY WELL, ARDMORE, CO. WATERFORD

—Exactly. A lot of people thought that was a very sound policy—that it brought people more quickly and easily to Christianity than would otherwise have happened. This sort of pragmatism, however, did not sit well with Puritans and Calvinists. They believed that if the Bible did not strictly direct something, it should not be part of the Christian religion.

16. But what happened to the cult of Mithras? I know that Christianity was legalized in Rome early in the fourth century and paganism was banned near the end of the fourth century, but

how do you ban a religion to which most of the army belongs? And how would the cult of Mithras have gone away so quietly that I've never even heard of it?

—There are plenty of theories about that, but it's not a subject on which it is easy to get hard information. One theory (believed by many, but which others find objectionable) is that the two religions, in effect, merged and that the influence of Mithraism is still clearly visible—in the all-male celibate clergy in the Catholic Church, for instance, perhaps in church vestments, and in the title 'Father' for priests.

EPIPHANY GIFTS (GOLD, FRANKINCENSE & MYRRH) BEING PRESENTED AT THE CHAPEL ROYAL IN 1902 (*I.L.N.*)

17. Why would that have happened?

—Imperial pressure might have brought it about, possibly the result of a process started by Constantine. By the fourth century, the Empire was shaky enough without a struggle between two significant religions adding to its problems.

18. That's all very murky.

MEDALLION OF CONSTANTINE WITH *SOL INVICTUS*

—Yes, but remember, we are just in the world of informed speculation here. Little documentary evidence is available to researchers about Mithraism (which is said to have been a mystery cult, its secrets revealed only to its initiates).

19. What about physical evidence?

—Excellent physical evidence of the cult can be

found all over the area of the Roman Empire, but it is not definitively informative about the cult's beliefs.

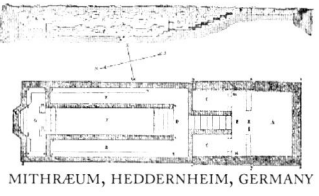

MITHRÆUM, HEDDERNHEIM, GERMANY

Chapter 9

The Banning of Christmas

The cult's equivalent of a church was a rectangular underground room called a *Mithraeum*, and the remains of these—often almost intact—have been discovered virtually everywhere there were Roman soldiers. There is an interesting one deep under the Basilica of San Clemente in Rome (it is four layers down, with three churches built over it); there is one in central London; the one pictured *[right >]* is one of several along Hadrian's Wall in the U.K.

MITHRÆUM NEAR NEWCASTLE, NORTH-EAST ENGLAND

20. O.K. Interesting. But back to Geneva. Did they keep the ban on Christmas there anyway, in spite of the violence it provoked?

—What seems to have happened is that, for the rest of Calvin's time there, Geneva settled into a minor church acknowledgment of Christmas (not on Christmas Day itself, however, but on the Sunday before or after December 25th).

21. What did Calvin think of that?

—In the aftermath of the trouble caused by the ban, Calvin took a classic lawyer's position about its imposition, saying—on the one hand—that if he had been asked he might have advised against it, but—on the other hand—he was glad it

CALVIN'S CHAIR IN ST PIERRE CHURCH, GENEVA

had been imposed:

> Although I have not been the mover nor instigator to it, yet, since it has so happened, I am not sorry for it.

22. I see.

—It appears Calvin was worried that the depth of fury felt by some Genevans about the banning of Christmas would threaten the strength of the Calvinist position there in Geneva (and might even drive people back to Catholicism). He wrote in 1555:

> Here is what has resulted [from the ban]. Not a year has passed without some quarrel and bickering, because the people were divided, and to such a degree as to draw their swords.

'COMMENCEMENT OF THE QUARREL' (J. PETTIE, C.1880)

23. What finally happened?

'SWORD & DAGGER FIGHT' (J. PETTIE, 1877)

—Near the end of the 17th century, Genevan authorities overruled Calvinist objection and declared Christmas a civil holiday.

'CHRISTMAS IN SWITZERLAND - A FANCY HEAD-DRESS DANCE - THE SERVANTS FINISH THE EVENING' (*THE GRAPHIC*, 1910)

Chapter 9

The Banning of Christmas

24. And Scotland—is it true that Christmas did not become a public holiday there until 1958?

—Yes. It was an ordinary working day.

BUSINESS LUNCH ON CHRISTMAS DAY - 'TURKEY'S OFF, SIR' (*I.L.N.*, 1880)

25. Was that for the same religious reasons as in Geneva?

—Pretty much. Presbyterianism had taken a quick and deep hold there under the leadership of John Knox.

JOHN KNOX (J. HONDIUS 1602)

26. So did anyone celebrate Christmas in Scotland before 1958?

'CHRISTMAS MORNING' (B.FOSTER, 1869)

—Yes, some did, but many preferred to ignore the holiday; and in the years when Knox's influence was fresh, the Church of Scotland had made a good effort to eradicate Christmas entirely. In 1560, its *First Book of Discipline* sought civil punishment for anyone who maintained the 'abominations' of 'Christmass' or 'Epiphany' and other holy days. In 1575 its General Assembly sought the abolition of those holy days:

> ... and a civil penalty against the keepers thereof by ceremonies, banqueting, fasting, and such other vanities.

Keeping Christmas Well

27. So they were nearly as strict in Scotland as in Geneva?

—In consistency of opposition to Christmas, even stricter. By 1590, because Calvin's own church of Geneva had been forced to relent sufficiently that it acknowledged the existence of Easter (*Pasche*) and Christmas (while still forbidding their celebration) King James VI of Scotland (who would later become King James I of England, and change his religious views) had this criticism to make of the Geneva church at the General Assembly of the Church of Scotland:

JOHN KNOX HOUSE, EDINBURGH (*ENGR.* 1829)

'The Kirk of Geneva keeps Pasche and Yule, what have they for them?' he asked reproachfully, to which the response was fifteen minutes of applause and prayers by the Assembly.

28. Did the Church of Scotland ever change its position?

—Time worked certain changes— in both church and state. In 1645 the General Assembly of the Church of Scotland was still keeping a very strict position. It voted that members found keeping Christmas could absolve themselves only by public repentance before the congregation.

INTERIOR OF CHURCH, VIZETELLY, 1851

By the 18th century (1713 and 1714) some signs of Christmas had reappeared. The courts of law, for instance, were taking a holiday at Christmas—the *'Yule vacance'* had been restored. Members of the Church of Scotland formally protested.

By 1731, the Church of Scotland itself was being criticized (by dissenting members) for tolerating Christmas. The dissenters were demanding that the Church enforce its own 1645 Act, and require public repentance of church members found to be observing Christmas:

> ...Masters of Schools and Colleges are accessory to this superstitious prophanity—by granting Liberty or Vacancy to their Scholars

'SCHOOL HOLIDAYS' (E.FRERE *I.L.N.*, 1876) >

> at such Times [Christmas]. But even the Elders of this Church, in many places, are guilty of observing Yule ... and yet never one of these censured, but connived at.

Revealingly, in relation to things to come, the dissenters go on to complain:

> ...a young up-rising Generation are left in Ignorance about the Sinfulness of that [Christmas], and other superstitious Days, too much in Fashion in our declining Days.

CHRISTMAS HOLIDAYS (J. LEECH *I.L.N.*, 1855)

Chapter 9

The Banning of Christmas

29. I see.

—Still, even in the strictest of times, some Scots just continued with cheerful Old Christmas habits. In 1605, five Aberdonians were brought before the Kirk session for going through the town 'maskit and dancing with bellis.' [—*Scotsman*]

'CHRISTMAS IN ADVERSITY' (*I.L.N.*, 1900)

30. It must have been a relief when Christmas was finally made a public holiday in 1958.

—Not to everyone. In 1962, the Free Presbyterian Church of Scotland issued a document in which it stated:
> The Free Presbyterian Church rejects the modern custom becoming so prevalent in the Church of Scotland of observing Christmas and Easter.

31. So what happened in 1958 that caused it to be made a public holiday?

—Some suggest that the shake-up of World War II had started or accelerated a change of attitude towards
CHRISTMAS TREE ON THE MOUND, EDINBURGH, PRESENTED BY NORWAY FOR SCOTLAND'S HELP IN WORLD WAR II
the holiday (and in every part of the world that recognized Christmas, the post-World-War-II years were a real high point for it). On 26th December 1950, the *Scotsman* newspaper reported

on the previous Christmas Day in Edinburgh: Everywhere in the city, the increasing observance of Christmas has been noted. The citizens were early abroad, quite a number of them making their way homewards during the first hour of the day, returning from carol services and midnight services at various city churches, their way in Princes Street at least lighted by Christmas trees.

CHRISTMAS STREET (LEECH, *I.L.N.*, 1850)

Chapter 9

The Banning of Christmas

The same newspaper quoted the Royal Chaplain, Dr Charles Warr, as saying that while Christmas was 'still largely unobserved as a religious festival in many parts of Scotland,' it 'was rapidly coming into its own again and was likely to supplant New Year's Day, which had no religious significance at all, in the affection of the Scottish people.'

New Year, however, was, and remains, the really important holiday in Scotland, with January 2nd also a public holiday.

'NEW YEAR'S EVE IN EDINBURGH' (W.B.MURRAY, *I.L.N.*, 1876)

32. In England, Christmas wasn't banned for all that long was it?

—No. In England (unlike in Scotland) mainstream Anglicans (rather than Puritan-leaning Anglicans or Calvinists) formed the majority of the population, and Anglicans (along with Lutherans and Catholics) celebrated Christmas. From 1640, however, Puritans (whose most prominent and influential member was Oliver Cromwell) effectively controlled the English parliament, and the Christmas holiday was in the sights of that Puritan-controlled Parliament from the beginning.

ENGLAND'S 'OLD FATHER CHRISTMAS' (*ROBIN RANGER'S PICTURE BOOK*, N.Y., 1865)

33. What did it do?

—In 1642, the Puritans introduced a monthly fast day, on the last Wednesday of every month. In 1644, Christmas fell on the last Wednesday of the month, and Parliament ordered that the fast was to be kept 'with the more solemn humiliation' on that account. This Parliamentary Order of 19th December, 1644 had no kind words to say about the holiday of Christmas:

OLIVER CROMWELL (S. COOPER C.1657)

> Whereas some doubts have been raised, whether the next fast shall be celebrated, because it falls on the day which heretofore was usually called the feast of the nativity of our Saviour, the lords and commons… do order and ordain, that public notice be given, that the fast appointed to be kept the last Wednesday in every month ought to be observed, till it be otherwise ordered by both houses; and that this day in particular is to be kept with the more solemn humiliation, because it may call to remembrance our sins, and the sins of our forefathers, who have turned this feast, pretending the memory of Christ, into an extreme forgetfulness of him, by giving liberty to carnal and spiritual delights, being contrary to the life which Christ led here on earth…

'PRIZE MEAT AT CHRISTMAS' (*I.L.N.*, 1843)

34. How did that go down?

—Not well. According to Daniel Neal's History of the Puritans (1837), non-Puritans 'raised loud clamours …as what had never been heard before in the Christian world.'

Chapter 9

The Banning of Christmas

'MARKETING AT CHRISTMAS TIME' (*ILLUSTRATED TIMES*, 1856)

35. So when did the Puritans actually ban Christmas?

—They banned it for the first time in 1645 (and they banned Easter and other holy days along with it). This is from the text of the order:

> Forasmuch as the feast of the nativity of Christ, Easter, Whitsuntide and other festivals, commonly called holy days, have been heretofore superstitiously used and observed, be it ordained that the said feasts, and all other festivals, commonly called holy days be no longer observed as festivals; …

'SHOPPING ON CHRISTMAS EVE' (EDW. & GEO. DALZIEL, 1850)

Keeping Christmas Well

36. Was that unpopular too?

—People in Canterbury *'had their heads broke'* in the rioting it provoked. The Sheriff of Canterbury, and other city officials trying to enforce the ban, were among those injured. Puritan shopkeepers who treated Christmas Day as a shopping day came under attack. Their windows were smashed and their goods thrown into the street. (In fact, heads were probably 'broke' in other places too, but the riot in Canterbury is best remembered because a vivid written record of it was left behind).

'FETCHING CHRISTMAS DINNER FROM THE BAKER'S OVEN' (E.&G.DALZIEL, 1850)

37. Did the ban affect Christmas religious ceremonies?

—There was a ban on religious services on Christmas day. The diarist, John Evelyn—who was arrested while attending a service at a chapel in the Strand in London on Christmas Day 1657—recorded:

JOHN EVELYN (H. VAN DER BORCHT 1641)

> These wretched miscreants, held their muskets against us as we came up to receive the Sacred Elements, as if they would have shot us at the Altar.

He was later released.

In 1647, the parish officers of St Margaret's, Westminster, had been arrested and fined because there had been preaching in that Church on Christmas Day and also because the church had been decorated with Christmas greenery.

38. Christmas greenery? You mean like holly and ivy? You weren't allowed to put up holly and ivy?

—No. In some places where it was put up, officials burned it. A 17th century writer, John Taylor, nicely caught the sense of popular outrage about this law, saying of the Puritans:

'DECORATING THE CHURCH FOR CHRISTMAS' (T. ONWHYN, 1843)

Chapter 9

The Banning of Christmas

—their madness hath extended itself to the very vegetables; senseless trees, herbs, and weeds, are in a profane estimation amongst them— holly, ivy, mistletoe, rosemary, bays, are accounted ungodly branches of superstition for your entertainment. And to roast a collar of beef, to touch a collar of brawn, to take a pie, to put a plum in the pottage pot, to burn a great candle, or to lay one block the more in the fire ... is enough to make a man to be suspected and taken for a Christian, for which he shall be apprehended for committing high Parliament Treason ...

GATHERING CHRISTMAS GREENERY (*I.L.N.*, 1871)

Keeping Christmas Well

RIGHT:
'THE MISTLETOE SELLER'
(PHIZ, *ILLUSTRATED LONDON NEWS*, 1853)

BELOW:
'THE HOLLY WAGON'
(B.FOSTER, *ILLUSTRATED LONDON NEWS*, 1848)

RIGHT:
'MISTLETOE GATHERER'
(*ILLUSTRATED LONDON NEWS*, 1894)

BELOW:
'BURNING THE CHRISTMAS GREENERY ON CANDLEMAS EVE'
(*THE GRAPHIC*, 1876)

Chapter 9

The Banning of Christmas

39. They really threw themselves into banning Christmas, didn't they?

'DISAPPEARANCE OF THE PLUM PUDDING' (*CHRISTMAS COMES BUT ONCE A YEAR*, EDW. & GEO. DALZIEL, 1850)

—Yes, although it was obviously hard to kill, because the Puritan Parliament felt the need to pass two more orders abolishing it, first on 3rd June 1647, and then on Christmas Eve 1652, when it proclaimed:

> no observance shall be had of the five and twentieth day of December, commonly called Christmas Day; nor any solemnity used or exercised in churches upon that day in respect thereof.

40. A lot of people must have been glad when the Puritans lost power.

THE TABLE OF SAMUEL PEPYS (*CHRISTMASTIDE, ITS HISTORY, FESTIVITIES, & CAROLS*, SANDYS, 1852)

—It seems so. Shortly after the Puritan regime ended, Samuel Pepys gave a nice account of the 'pleasure' and 'content' he felt at being able to enjoy simple traditional comforts on Christmas Day. He started the day with a religious service and then:

> I walked home again with great pleasure, and there dined by my wife's bed-side with great content, having a mess of brave plum-porridge and a roasted pullet for dinner, and I sent for a mince-pie abroad, my wife not being well to make any herself yet. [*Thursday 25 December 1662*]

Keeping Christmas Well

41. But the Puritans' ban had a lasting effect all the same, even after it was lifted?

—It did really. Even though Christmas was being celebrated again, two decades of anti-Christmas propaganda (in which words such as 'demonic' and 'Popish' were regularly applied to the holiday and to those who kept it) left a legacy.

'A CHRISTMAS HYMN' (JACOVACE, *I.L.N.*, 1889)

The English Christmas never again regained the exuberance with which it had been celebrated before the Puritan and Oliver Cromwell years, and it is interesting to note how much defensiveness and religious apologizing crept into books published in England about Christmas and Christmas traditions written in the centuries after the ban.

42. What do you mean?

—The following account was written by Anglican curate Henry Bourne in 1725. Commenting on the popular celebration of Christmas, he is nearly as censorious in tone as the Calvinist Philip Stubbes had been a century and a half earlier:

> Such I am afraid had been the Observation of the Christmas Holy-days…the generality of Men have rather look'd upon them as a Time of Eating

'CHRISTMAS DINNER' (G. CRUIKSHANK, 1835)

and Drinking and Playing, than of returning Praises and Thanksgivings to God, for the greatest Benefit he ever bestowed upon the Sons of Men.

43. I see.

—The same John Evelyn who had broken the law to attend a Christmas service in 1657 was driven to complain to his diary in 1662 about a church sermon in which the congregation had been preached to on 'how to behave ourselves in festival rejoicing.'

'THE LONG CHRISTMAS SERMON - WATCHING THE CLOCK'
(FRANK LESLIE'S ILLUSTRATED NEWS, 1887)

Even though the Puritans had gone from power, it seemed they left behind them (at least in part of the public mind) a changed attitude towards Christmas: the wholehearted celebration of it was just not as 'respectable' as it had been in the past.

44. Did the Puritans ban Christmas in the U.S. as well?

—Yes, in Massachusetts. The celebration of Christmas was made an offence there in 1659. Anyone staying away from work or found feasting on Christmas Day would be fined five shillings. A second five shilling fine was imposed on anyone found gambling with cards or dice.

45. Did people mind?

—In general, no. It was a popular ban. As in Scotland, a majority of the population in Massachusetts did not want to celebrate Christmas. Their opposition to Christmas was visible from the moment they arrived in the New World.

46. What do you mean?

'THE PURITAN GOVERNOR INTERRUPTS THE CHRISTMAS SPORTS' (H. PYLE, 1883)

—The master of the *Mayflower*, Christopher Jones (who was not a Puritan), recorded how resolutely his passengers ignored the holiday:

> At anchor in Plymouth Harbour; Christmas Day, but not observed by these colonists, they being opposed to all saints' days… No man rested all that day.

47. How long did the ban last?

CHRISTMAS MORNING (DODGSON, *I.L.N.* 1846)

—Until 1681. But the Puritan colonists didn't repeal the ban willingly. This was a measure forced on them by London, and it caused much bad feeling.

48. So did the colonists ignore Christmas then by choice, after there was no longer a law against it?

—Most did ignore it, but a minority (mainly Anglicans and Lutherans) started celebrating

Christmas as soon as they could.

'CHRISTMAS DINNER' (E. & G. DALZIEL, *CHRISTMAS COMES BUT ONCE A YEAR*, 1850)

Chapter 9

The Banning of Christmas

In 1687, the Rev. Increase Mather wrote disapprovingly about these 'Christmas-keepers,' as he termed them:

INCREASE MATHER

> How few are there comparatively that spend those Holidays (as they are called) after a Holy manner. But they are consumed in Compotations, in Interludes, in playing at Cards, in Revellings, in excess of Wine, in mad Mirth...

'CHRISTMAS MERRYMAKING IN THE 17th CENTURY' (*THE GRAPHIC*, 1875)

By 1712, his son Cotton Mather, was finding the 'Christmas-keepers' as unrepentant as ever:

COTTON MATHER 1728

> The Feast of Christ's Nativity is spent in Reveling, Dicing, Carding, Masking, and in Licentious Liberty... by Mad Mirth, by long Eating, by hard Drinking, by lewd Gaming, by rude Reveling...

49. I see.

—There was nothing much new in their complaint. They sounded a bit like the first millennium Catholic Church, and like the 16th century Calvinist Philip Stubbes, who had made the following observation in 1583:

'PUTTING UP THE HOLLY & MISTLETOE' (*I.L.N.* 1855)

Especially in Christmas time there is nothing else used but cards, dice, tables, masking, mumming, bowling, and such like fooleries; and the reason is, that they think they have a commission and prerogative that time to do what they list, and to follow what vanity they will. But (alas!) do they think that they are privileged at that time to do evil? …who knows not that more mischief is that time committed than in all the year besides?

REMINISCING AT CHRISTMAS (*LL.N.*, 1873)

50. They really were obsessed with Christmas, weren't they?

—Well yes, but for those people who had severe

views about religion, or were very hierarchical, or liked great order in their lives, the old European Christmas must have been a yearly trial.

51. What do you mean?

—Not only were the conventions about disregarding hierarchy very strong, but it also was close to an official requirement that the population in general act nonsensically over Christmas. There were customs such as the 'Feast of Fools' (very important in France) and the 'Boy Bishop' *[right>]* (significant on the continent and in England) which involved, to varying degrees, religious ceremonies being ridiculed. One of the most extraordinary conventions of the pre-Puritan Christmas was the official appointment of 'Lords of Misrule' for the season that ran from Halloween to Candlemas.

MEDIEVAL 'BOY BISHOP' (*WEBSTER*)

Chapter 9

The Banning of Christmas

52. I'm still not sure I understand what the 'Lord of Misrule' did.

—He was a sort of specialised entertainments director for Christmas, whose job was to arrange nonsense. If you can imagine hiring one of the Marx brothers to take charge of your Christmas, that seems to have been both the aim and the effect of appointing a Lord of Misrule.

Every household of substance appointed a Lord of Misrule; the universities of Oxford and Cambridge had Lords of Misrule. The Mayor of London and the Sheriffs each had

GROUCHO AS RUFUS T. FIREFLY (*DUCK SOUP*, 1933, DIRECTOR: LEO M^cCAREY)

one, and these competed with one another for 'who should make the rarest pastime to delight the beholders.' [—Ellis] Their rule extended from All Hallows Eve until Candlemas Day,

> in which space there were fine and subtle disguisings, masks and mummeries, with playing at cards in every house, more for pastimes than for gaine. [—Ellis]

53. O.K.

—Also, to be appointed Lord of Misrule (in the time before the Puritans came to power) was a great honour. His powers then were taken pretty seriously. When he commanded nonsense to be performed, it was something of an obligation.

'LORD OF MISRULE'
(ENGR. W.B.SCOTT, 1850)

54. What do you mean?

—Sir Walter Scott, for instance, gave an account of an official in Scotland who had been sent in 1547 to the residence of a Lord Borthwick for the serious purpose of serving Letters of Excommunication on him. When the official arrived, however, it was the Christmas season, and Lord Borthwick's 'Abbot of Unreason' [the Scottish title for the Lord of Misrule] had charge of household. By command of the Abbot of Unreason, the official was seized, ducked, forced to eat the parchment Letters of Excommunication (which had been soaked in wine) and then to drink the wine.

WALTER SCOTT
(H. RAEBURN 1815)

It was not always thus : there was a season When Christmas had its Abbot of Unreason
ABBOT OF UNREASON (1850, RECOLLECTIONS OF OLD CHRISTMAS)

55. Goodness.

—Shortly afterwards (in 1555) Calvinist Scotland banned the appointment of Abbots of Unreason.

56. So was the Lord of Misrule custom killed off in the time of the Puritans?

BRINGING IN YULE LOG UNDER DIRECTION OF LORD OF MISRULE
(E.MONTEFIORE, *ILLUSTRATED SPORTING & DRAMATIC NEWS*, 1890)

Chapter 9

The Banning of Christmas

—Not exactly, although it seems to have been fatally weakened. It did reappear afterwards, but then faded away very quickly. At the Inns of Court, for instance, traditionally it had been a great honour to be appointed Lord of Misrule (and their Lords of Misrule had been responsible for some notorious episodes). By the end of the 17th century, however, a financial inducement was needed to get someone to take up the job. The records of Gray's Inn in 1682, for instance, indicate that a Mr Richard Gipps agreed to take the job only on the basis that his dues for the next term would be waived.

LONDON LORD OF MISRULE PARADE (SANDYS, *CHRISTMASTIDE*, 1852)

57. What notorious episodes?

—In 1627, one of their Lords of Misrule led a group late at night on Twelfth Eve to break down the doors of houses of nearby streets, claiming a rent of five shillings from each house. He was arrested eventually (by a party led by the Lord Mayor) but only after blows were struck. The mediation of the Attorney General was required for his release.

A few years earlier, also on Twelfth Day, in 1622, a group from Gray's Inn, took four cart-loads of 'chambers' (short cannons used for celebrations) from the Tower of London, shot them, woke the city and the king, who is said to have jumped out of bed, shouting 'treason.'

GRAY'S INN BARRISTER IN 17th CENTURY COSTUME, WITH LORD OF MISRULE HOBBYHORSE, AT A MASQUE HELD IN GRAY'S INN, LONDON, IN 1887 (*I.L.N.*, 1887)

58. I see. So the Calvinist Philip Stubbes wasn't really exaggerating when he said that, at Christmas—

there is nothing else but cards, dice, tables, masking, bowling and such like fooleries; and the reason is that they think they have a commission and prerogative that time to do what they list, and to follow what vanity they will.

—No, he wasn't really. The old European

'CHRISTMAS BREAK - PLAYING CARDS' (C. LARSSON, 1909)

Christmas was a public party of an extravagance that is now hard to imagine. It was governed principally by the rule that there should be no rules, except the one requiring the rich and the powerful to share and to be generous.

185

Chapter 9

The Banning of Christmas

THE CHRISTMAS DOLE (G.DODGSON, *ILN.*, 1856)

59. I still find it hard to understand why that manner of celebrating Christmas—as a great communal public holiday—survived for so long and then was forgotten, and why Christmas itself almost died in places.

—O.K. In chapter eleven—why Christmas almost died (in the English-speaking world)—after another interlude chapter.

'AN OLD-TIME CHRISTMAS REVEL' (GLADMAN, *I.L.N.*, 1900)

CHAPTER 10

—*Interlude*—
More Movies for Christmas

OUTSIDE MATUSCHEK'S IN BUDAPEST
[*THE SHOP AROUND THE CORNER*]

The Shop Around the Corner

The Shop Around the Corner, 1940 (D.: Ernst Lubitsch).
 An oddly addictive, unusual film. Set in a leather-goods shop in pre-war middle Europe, *The Shop Around the Corner* nicely evokes a sense of time and place; and the small specialized world in which it is set becomes the whole world. See it once, and you'll find yourself wanting to see it again. Although its values are those of the world of commerce, somehow it makes you feel that the commercial side of Christmas is not all bad.
 Alfred (James Stewart), the manager of

187

Chapter 10

Interlude

More Movies for Christmas

the shop and Klara (Margaret Sullivan), hired as a sales assistant, are lonely-hearts penpals and admirers of one another's anonymous correspondence. In person, they annoy one another. [The film was remade in 1998 in a New York setting as *You've Got Mail*.] The owner of the shop tries to take his own life after learning that his wife has been unfaithful. As a present to him, the shop workers decide to try to clear the shelves of stock on Christmas Eve. They succeed. At closing time, the owner visits the shop and hands out generous bonuses. The romantic plot between Alfred and Klara resolves itself. The owner, now on his own for Christmas, invites the newly hired messenger boy (also on his own) for a proper Budapest Christmas Eve dinner:

MIKULÁS, THE HUNGARIAN ST NICHOLAS, WITH GIFTS TO PUT IN SHOES LEFT OUT BY CHILDREN (BUDAPEST, E.BENEDEK 1859-1929)

'... Do you like chicken noodle soup? What would you think of roast goose stuffed with baked apples and fresh boiled potatoes and butter and some red cabbage on the side? —and then some cucumber salad with sour cream? —and then a double order of apple-strudel with vanilla sauce?'
—Mmm.

IT'S A WONDERFUL LIFE

It's a Wonderful Life, 1946 (Director: Frank Capra).

Regarded by many as the quintessential Christmas movie, it leaves only the stonehearted dry-eyed at its end. Although not a perfect film, its weak spots are in the first half, and it finishes so brilliantly that you forgive and forget its flaws—principally the drawn-out courtship scenes between Donna Reed and a 38-year-old  James Stewart, who looked his age, but played (in those scenes) a boy barely out of his teens.

The film was not a commercial success when first released, and attained its current, revered status in the 1970s and 1980s (during what amounted to a gap period in the film's copyright protection) when it was shown repeatedly on television over the Christmas season. Emotionally memorable moments are when a despairing George Bailey (James Stewart) is shown the honky-tonk hell his nice small town would have become if he had never been born, and, of course, when the whole town shows up to save him at  the end of the film. A visually memorable moment is when a 1946 high-school gym floor opens to reveal a swimming pool underneath: this was filmed in a real gym—at Beverly Hills High School.

Chapter 10

Interlude

More Movies for Christmas

Prancer, 1989 (Director: John Hancock).

Very real, immensely charming. Everything about this film (set in farming, small-town Midwest) seems so without artifice— the children (in particular Rebecca Harrell as 9-year-old Jessica); the teachers (Marcia Porter—a very realistic Mrs Fairburn); the town's ancient set of Christmas decorations that falls apart; the financial stresses of farm life—that you have no problem believing the injured reindeer (found and hidden by Jessica), who proves to have a passion for Christmas cookies, is the genuine Prancer.

Trading Places, 1983 (Director: John Landis). A very funny movie set over the Christmas season (with Dan Aykroyd, Eddie Murphy, Jamie Lee Curtis, and Denholm Elliott) which, by accident or by design, includes a huge number of the Roman customs  that were incorporated into Christmas, including the tradition of the rich and the poor trading

places, and the wearing of costumes and animal masks. It is probably fair to say that no other film has made quite such effective use of an animal costume for the resolution of a plot.

Chapter 10

Interlude

More Movies for Christmas

Junior Miss, 1945 (Director: George Seaton).

Ignore the (lightweight) plot if you like, and watch this as a snapshot of family life in a Manhattan apartment in the 1940s, at a time when there was an actual transition between childhood and adolescence (the first pair of high heels, given as a Christmas present, is a coming-of-age moment). The comfortably-off family live realistically in a tiny apartment (the two daughters have a boundary line down the middle of their small room) and skating in Rockefeller Center *[right >]* is an important part of adolescent culture.

The world-of-their-own bubble in which 13-year-old girls live is perceptively caught. There is some very smart dialogue in the film, which was a successful stage play; and, as with *The Thin Man*, there was no taboo on drinking too much. The two 13-year-old girls, Judy (Peggy Ann Garner) and Fuffy (Barbara Whiting), take for granted that their parents (their fathers in particular) will be

badly hung over on New Year's morning. The film has a truly great scene about the hazards of hiding from an unwanted visitor. [Unfortunately, not available on DVD (or VHS) at time of writing.]

NOT AT HOME TO AN UNWANTED VISITOR

JUDY & ELLEN (FAYE MARLOWE) AT THE ROCKEFELLER CENTER SKATING RINK IN *JUNIOR MISS*, 1945

YOUNG SKATERS AT ROCKEFELLER CENTER, NEW YORK, CHRISTMAS 1941 (*PHOTO:* JOHN COLLIER)

CHRISTMAS 1943 – ROCKEFELLER CENTER SKATING RINK (*PHOTO:* LIBRARY OF CONGRESS)

THE HOLLY AND THE IVY

Chapter 10

Interlude

More Movies for Christmas

The Holly and the Ivy, 1952 (Director: George More O'Ferrall).

Hollywood has something of a monopoly on great, non-Scrooge Christmas movies, but this is an interesting, peaceful English film from the early 1950s —

well-acted and for grown-ups. Ralph Richardson plays a small-town parson; Jenny (Celia Johnson) is his stay-at-home daughter (who would like to move to South America with the man who wants to marry her); Margaret (Margaret Leighton) is his London-resident daughter with a past; Michael (Denholm Elliott), his son in the army; and together with

their two very different aunts (one grand, one not) they come home for Christmas. Not exciting, but calm and comfortable.

Keeping Christmas Well

THE BELLS OF ST. MARY'S

The Bells of St. Mary's, 1945 (Dir.: Leo McCarey). This film gets its 'Christmas movie' credentials from its hilarious nativity play— genuinely improvised by very young non-actors. It also has one of the funniest scenes ever put on film—when a kitten gets under Fr O'Malley's (Bing Crosby's) hat *[>]*. A

huge hit when it was made (it was second in box office takings only to *Gone With the Wind*) this film became unfashionable with critics, although directors Frank Capra and Francis Ford Coppola paid homage to it—Diane Keaton and Al Pacino go to see the film in

The Godfather; and when James Stewart's town becomes wholesome again in *It's a Wonderful Life*, the film playing in the town's cinema is *The Bells of St. Mary's*.

Director Leo McCarey (who, along with his close friend Hal Roach, is said to

be responsible for the teaming of Laurel and Hardy) was a great believer in improvisation. He cast the young son of the film's musical director as Joseph in the nativity play, and let him ad-lib his lines.

JOSEPH STRUGGLES TO LIFT MARY ONTO THE DONKEY

Joseph first introduces Mary (who is bigger than he is) and then gamely (but with difficulty) lifts her on to the wooden donkey. He knocks on 'doors' asking if they can have a place to stay for the night, and when one of the 'innkeepers' replies too quickly that he and Mary can't stay because they don't have any money, Joseph points out: 'I didn't even ask you yet. Go back and start again.' The baby Jesus (played by an 18-month toddler) makes a bolt from the stage *[>]* before his big moment—when the children surround the clothes basket in which he is sitting to sing 'Happy Birthday' to him *[>]*.

THE BABY JESUS ESCAPES

A quote from Leo McCarey:
> I'll let someone else photograph the ugliness of the world. It's larceny to remind people of how lousy things are and call it entertainment.

Chapter 10

Interlude

More Movies for Christmas

Bad Santa

Bad Santa, 2003 (Director: Terry Zwigoff).
For the most part, we are not listing very recent movies that everyone knows about anyway, but we are including this one, because it has surprising depths—and courage! (It is

SANTA'S TRANSPORT SUFFERS A BREAKDOWN (C.D. GIBSON, 1904)

'SANTA TAKES A LIFT IN A NEW OLDSMOBILE' (E. PENFIELD, 1906)

not however a Santa movie for children young enough to believe.) This film is about innocence (the hopeless 'Kid' played by Brett Kelly); about uncomplicated decency (the Mrs Santa's Sister who asks no questions); about politically incorrect evil (the dwarf is the villain?!!!); about a scene that comes out of nowhere (young children scream when they see Santa being shot by police as he delivers a present); and about redemption—maybe nobody except Billy Bob Thornton could pull off such a convincing transformation, but he succeeds.

Chapter 10

Interlude

More Movies for Christmas

BAD SANTA & MRS SANTA'S SISTER

FINALLY, TWO ANIMATED FILMS:

THE NIGHTMARE BEFORE CHRISTMAS

The Nightmare Before Christmas, 1993 (Writer & Producer: Tim Burton).

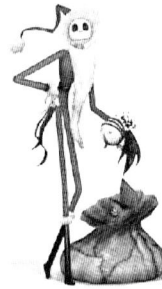

A highly imaginative stop-action movie. It captures the beyond-our-understanding appeal of Christmas—so potent that it seduces even The Halloween Pumpkin King. Both revolutionary and full of heart.

Keeping Christmas Well

LADY AND THE TRAMP

Lady and the Tramp, 1955 (Walt Disney Studios).

If Christmas hasn't gone as peacefully or cheerfully as you'd like, put on this film—a great one to watch if life is going against you and you need perking up. It's probably the most satisfying full-length animated film ever made. It's smart, funny and pretty; stray

dog Peg (Peggy Lee) sings 'He's a Tramp, but I Love Him'; it begins and ends at Christmas; and jaded

adults will enjoy it as much as tiny children. Unless you really hate dogs, always have a copy of this film in the house.

CHAPTER 11

THE RESURGENT CHRISTMAS OF THE ENGLISH-SPEAKING WORLD

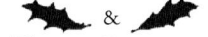

THE THREE REVOLUTIONS THAT (ALMOST) KILLED IT

Up to the latter part of the last century ... carols were sung in Churches on Christmas Day, and in private houses on Christmas Eve throughout the West of England.

—Those words were written in 1822 by Davies Gilbert, who was recalling for 19th century readers the antiquated, largely forgotten custom of singing Christmas carols. The title *[>]* alone

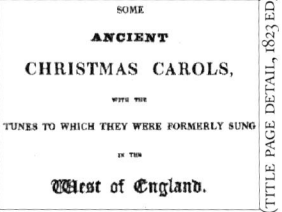

(TITLE PAGE DETAIL, 1823 ED)

of Gilbert's landmark book, *Some Ancient Christmas Carols with the Tunes to which they were Formerly Sung in the West of England*, gives an idea of how obsolete the custom of singing carols already had become.

DAVIES GILBERT 1767-1839

Among the 'ancient' carols preserved by Gilbert's work were 'Whilst Shepherds Watch'd Their Flocks by Night' *[below]*, and 'The First Nowell' (in the 1823 second edition).

A decade later, antiquarian William Sandys listed the few pockets where the practice of

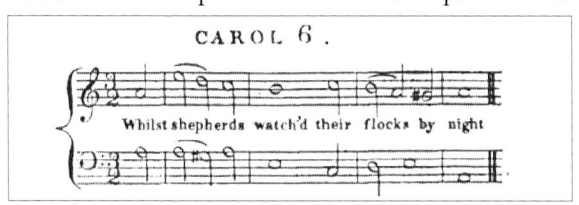

'WHILST SHEPHERDS...' (1823 MUSIC ARRANGEMENT)

carol-singing had survived in England:

> In the Northern counties, and in some of the midland, carol-singing is still preserved. In the metropolis, a solitary itinerant may be occasionally heard in the streets, croaking out 'God Rest You Merry, Gentlemen,' or some other old carol, to an ancient and simple tune. [*Christmas Carols Ancient and Modern*, 1833]

'THE STREET CAROL' (PHIZ, 1851)

1. When did carol singing become universal again?

—It took a while. In 1847, the *Illustrated London News* was still writing in the past tense about the practice in England:

> The Carol… is almost universally sung at Christmas, on the Continent. It is likewise sung

CAROLLERS BRINGING A CRIB IN RUSSIA (*THE GRAPHIC*, 1883)

in Ireland and in Wales, but in Scotland it is unknown. In various parts of England, within the present century, the singing of carols began on Christmas Eve, and was continued late into the night. On Christmas Day these Carols took

Chapter 11

The Resurgent Christmas of the English-speaking World

FISHERMAN, SPANISH BY DESCENT AND IN LIFESTYLE, BUT SETTLED IN BRIGHTON—'SAID TO BE THE DESCENDANTS OF A PARTY OF SPANISH REFUGEES WHO SETTLED THERE IN THE REIGN OF ELIZABETH'—CONTINUE THE NON-ENGLISH PRACTICE OF SINGING CAROLS AT CHRISTMAS (HINE, *I.L.N.*, 1849)

the place of Psalms in the churches, the whole congregation joining;...of late, there has been a sort of revival of taste for the Scriptural Carol. Last year, two or three reprinted collections appeared; one of them illuminated in gold and colour, after the manner of an ancient missal. [—*I.L.N.*, 1847]

CAROLLERS (PHIZ, 1855)

2. **Was it only in England that people more or less stopped celebrating Christmas?**

—What happened in England was extreme, with the evolution of Christmas there following a different path to that of any other European country. Perhaps most significantly, the change of tradition in England would, in turn, affect Christmas in America (which then, of course, would influence the world). Even in those parts of the U.S.

(for instance, in New York) where the European street-carnival Christmas briefly survived, this type of public celebrating (involving the principle that everyone was equal) was perceived as a threat by the powerful and the rich, who succeeded in putting an end to it. Before long, the American Christmas became the short, family-oriented (and commercial!) Christmas of today.

ABOVE: 'CHRISTMAS SHOPPING' (THE GRAPHIC, 1913)

ABOVE: 'CHRISTMAS ON FIFTH AVENUE' (A. BARBER, NEW YORK, 1896)

'CHRISTMAS TOYS IN MACY'S WINDOW, NEW YORK' C. 1910 (BAIN COLL.)

< THE OLD-FASHIONED CHRISTMAS-KEEPER & THE LATER, ABSTEMIOUS CHRISTMAS-KEEPER SHARE A TABLE (R.C. WOODVILLE, *I.L.N.* 1905)

Chapter 11

The Resurgent Christmas of the English-speaking World

3. It obviously took more than a few years of Puritan rule to have that great an effect. Was there some big change in the social order?

—A huge change. People use the word 'revolution' of three different historical developments in England that took place in the centuries when its Christmas almost died— the Agricultural Revolution, the Puritan Revolution, and the Industrial Revolution—and it is not an inappropriate or exaggerated word in relation to any of the three.

'THE CAVALIER'S TOAST' (*I.L.N.* 1897)

4. Well, I get the effect of the Puritans, but if any of the rest is relevant to Christmas, maybe

you'd better explain.

—O.K. Take the Agricultural Revolution first. This is shorthand for the ending (over many centuries) of the manorial system of land usage in England, one consequence of which was that a large number of agricultural tenants and labourers no longer had a living in the countryside.

BRINGING IN THE YULE LOG (*CHAMBERS' BOOK OF DAYS*, 1869)

5. **Um… what on earth does the 'manorial system'—whatever that means—or its ending, have to do with Christmas?**

LIGHTING THE YULE LOG (H.M.PAGET C.1900)

—Surprisingly, a lot. A big—really big—Christmas was more or less compulsory under the manorial system.

6. **So what was the 'manorial system'?**

—'The manor' was a farming unit, and also the equivalent of a little kingdom. There was the

'GATE OF THE OLD ENGLISH GENTLEMAN' (SEYMOUR, *BOOK OF CHRISTMAS*, 1836)

landlord and there were tenants. The land was divided into large open areas, and the arable part of it was farmed cooperatively by the tenants, each of whom had some rights over small strips of it.

7. OK. But about Christmas…?

—For the purposes of *this* book, the landlord had one role which was more significant than any other—he was the tenants' host at Christmas. And whatever else landlords did well or badly, they usually did a profoundly great job of hosting Christmas.

HOSTING CHRISTMAS (*RECOLLECTIONS OF OLD CHRISTMAS*, 1850)

8. What did they do?

—They hosted a celebration that was prolonged and communal, central to which was the preparation and consumption of mind-boggling quantities of food. There was an obligation on the powerful to provide a great feast and to share it—*in theory*, on a basis of equality—with all those who depended on them. Agricultural labourers appear to have been allowed almost a complete break from their ordinary working life. This arrangement was, in effect, obligatory in the countryside.

'BARONIAL HALL CHRISTMAS' (R. SEYMOUR, *BOOK OF CHRISTMAS*, 1836)

'BRINGING IN THE BOAR'S HEAD' (R. SEYMOUR, *BOOK OF CHRISTMAS*, 1836)

9. **How could that be?**

—It was part of preserving the system which (although as undemocratic as a system could be) at Christmas time seemed to work to the advantage of those at the lower end of the scale. In England, the law sometimes intervened to ensure that the poor in the countryside enjoyed a long and well-fed Christmas—that was how seriously the universal entitlement to a grand Christmas celebration was taken.

10. **How did the law do that?**

RETURNING HOME FOR CHRISTMAS (*I.L.N.* 1902)

Its interventions were pretty specific. In the 16th and 17th centuries, for instance, legal proclamations required people of means to return from London to their homes at Christmas, 'and there to keep hospitality among their neighbours.' Not long before the Puritans took over in the 17th century, Charles I ordered that

> ...every nobleman or gentleman, bishop, rector or curate, unless he be in the service of the Court or Council, shall... resort to their

several counties where they usually reside, and there keep their habitations and hospitality.

11. So the rich were breaking the law if they failed to feed and entertain the poor at Christmas?

Chapter 11

The Resurgent Christmas of the English-speaking World

ENGLISH COUNTRYSIDE IN 17th CENTURY - A DEPICTION IN *THE GENTLEWOMAN*, 1892

—At times and places, yes. The Christmas proclamation made in the reign of Elizabeth I is interesting for the portrait it paints of the late 16th century English countryside at Christmas. This proclamation commanded 'the nobility and gentry of Norfolk and Suffolk to leave London and return to their own counties before Christmas'—for the reason that the country alehouses at Christmas time were 'the resort of many idle strollers, under the guise of minstrels, jugglers, revellers, &c.' and the presence of the landlords might prevent trouble arising. [—Sandys]

12. The countryside was full of minstrels and jugglers?

—Apparently.

13. So the ideals set out by Dickens for the manner in which people should behave at Christmas had in fact been legal obligations, as well as widespread custom, just two centuries earlier?

—Yes. The following description (by a 19th century antiquarian) of a manorial Christmas in

Keeping Christmas Well

the early 17th century, is sanitized, patronizing, and deeply rose-tinted, but you cannot help but conclude that the Christmas celebrations were a pretty big deal for everyone involved:

The noblemen and gentry were…directed to return to their mansion houses in the country, to keep up hospitality during the Christmas; and many of them lived like petty princes, their household establishments forming almost a mimic court. The Christmas feast was kept up, the poor man's heart was cheered by earthly comforts … The great hall resounded with the mirth of the servants, and tenants, and other dependants, whose gambols amused the lord of the mansion, and his family and friends; and their presence and participation in the festivities, together with the shows exhibited by them, of which the poorer classes were frequently allowed to be the amused spectators, encouraged them, and mitigated the trials and privations of the winter. [—Sandys]

BRINGING IN THE BOAR'S HEAD (VIZETELLY, 1851)

A summer-green hung everywhere,
For Christmas came but once a year.
(*POEM:* T. MILLER; *DRAWING:* J. GILBERT, *CHRISTMAS POEMS & PICTURES*, N.Y., 1864)

14. So what did they get to eat?

—A lot usually. The following, is a description of the Christmas kept by a John Carminow of Cornwall 'about the time of Henry the Eighth':

PLUM PUDDING & BOAR'S HEAD
(RECOLLECTIONS OF OLD CHRISTMAS, 1850)

> He kept open house for all comers and goers, drinkers, minstrells, dancers, and what not, during the Christmas time, and… his usual allowance of provision for those twelve days, were twelve fat bullocks, twenty Cornish bushels of wheat, … thirty-six sheep, with hogs, lambs, and fowls, of all sort, and drink made of wheat and oat-malt proportionable. [—Sandys, 1833, quoting historian William Hals, 1655-1737.]

15. Did they keep to the Saturnalia/Kalends ideal that everyone was equal?

—As an ideal, yes. But it is clear from the amount of praise heaped on those households which put the ideal into practice that the great majority must have fallen short. Mill's *Age of Chivalry* praises Penshurst in Kent for *not* making use of a 'huge salt-cellar' to separate 'the noble from the ignoble guests' at Christmas in the 16th century

BANQUET IN PENSHURST HALL, KENT (J. NASH, 1838)

—leaving one with the impression that less idealistic establishments must have made use of such a barrier:

All who enjoyed the hospitality of Penshurst were equal in consideration of the host. There were no odious distinctions of rank or fortune; the dishes did not grow coarser as they receded from the head of the table, and no huge salt-cellar divided the noble from the ignoble guests.

SERVING THE GOOSE AT A 16th CENTURY CHRISTMAS BANQUET > (VIZETELLY, *CHRISTMAS WITH THE POETS*, 1851)

16. Interesting.

—Ben Johnson felt driven to pay tribute to the same family's hospitality with the following lines:

Whose liberal board doth flow
   With all that hospitality doth know!
Where comes no guest but is allowed to eat
   Without his fear, and of the Lord's own meat.
Where the same beer and bread, and self-same wine
   That is his lordship's, shall be also mine.

Again, by implication, it would seem that inferior bread, meat, and wine must have been the lot of guests at other houses.

CHRISTMAS IN 16th CENTURY ENGLAND (*LAROUSSE GASTRONOMIQUE*)

17. So in relation to the disappearance of Christmas in England…?

—Well, think of this sequence. In the 200 years following the Puritans' time in power, England changed beyond recognition. Landlords gradually (and to considerable public outcry) 'enclosed' all their land—i.e. created boundaries around and within it so that it was no longer farmed communally by many tenants. As a consequence, vast numbers of men, women, and children lost their living in the country, and communities disappeared.

18. That heartbreaking poem by Oliver Goldsmith, *The Deserted Village* was supposed to have been inspired by all that, wasn't it?

OLIVER GOLDSMITH (BY JOSHUA REYNOLDS 18th CENT.)

—Many people think so. Some have said he romanticized the rural life, but you have to love him for it:

> A time there was, ere England's grief began,
>   When every rood of ground maintain'd its man;
> For him light labour spread her wholesome store,
>   Just gave what life required, but gave no more:
> His best companions, innocence and health,
>   And his best riches, ignorance of wealth.
> But times are alter'd: trade's unfeeling train
>   Usurp the land, and dispossess the swain.

THE ANGEL OF DEATH HOVERS OVER THE DISPOSSESSED
—1800S ILLUSTRATION TO *THE DESERTED VILLAGE* (1770)

19. So what happened then?

—Skip on two centuries, and by the middle of the 19th century, England—after going through

Chapter 11

The Resurgent Christmas of the English-speaking World

the first and biggest industrial revolution in the world—had become a highly industrialized country.

20. That wasn't much good for Christmas, was it?

—It was a disaster for Christmas.

CHILD WORKERS IN MILL, 1840

21. I suppose it was inevitable. A long holiday in the middle of winter would cost the agricultural world very little, but it would cost industry a lot.

—Yes. And there may even be another dimension as well. Some historians make the interesting point that people whose ideology included a sincerely-felt disapproval of Christmas—i.e. people of Calvinist leanings—ended up in especially large numbers in trade and industry:

> During the first four decades of the seventeenth century... growing numbers of Englishmen, especially those who lived by trade and industry, came under Calvinistic influences. [*History of Western Civilization, A Handbook*, by Wm. H. McNeill, University of Chicago Press, 1969.]

'BUSINESSMAN'S CHRISTMAS DINNER' (*I.L.N.*, 1865)

22. You make it sound like it was practically a conspiracy of powerful forces against Christmas?

—Well, it's just a theory, of course. But it seems likely that if enough industrial capitalists were

'CRUSTY OLD BACHELORS' CHRISTMAS' (*ILLUSTRATED LONDON NEWS*, 1889)

Chapter 11

The Resurgent Christmas of the English-speaking World

hostile to Christmas for ideological or religious reasons, as well as because it interfered with their profits, it would go some ways towards explaining why the English Christmas went from being one of the biggest in the world to having a near-death experience.

23. When was the Industrial Revolution anyway?

—The Industrial Revolution started around 1750 (give or take a decade or two); and as a 'revolution' most say it had finished by 1850.

ABOVE: 'COALBROOKDALE BY NIGHT,' SHROPSHIRE (P.J. LOUTHERBOURG, 1801)

24. I see—at about the same time as they were starting to have to raffle off Twelfth Cakes to get rid of them?

—Yes.

Keeping Christmas Well

'OUTCASTS AT CHRISTMASTIME' (*ILLUSTRATED SPORTING & DRAMATIC NEWS*, LONDON, 1883)

'CHRISTMAS PARTY OUT IN THE COLD' (MULREADY, *ILLUSTRATED LONDON NEWS*, 1886)

'CHRISTMAS IN THE STREET—THE MATCH SELLER'
(F. BARRASO, *PICTORIAL WORLD*, LONDON, C. 1880)

Chapter 11

The Resurgent Christmas of the English-speaking World

'CHRISTMAS OUT OF DOORS' [WINSLOW HOMER, *HARPER'S WEEKLY*, U.S. 1858, *(BOSTON PUBLIC LIBRARY)*]

CHAPTER 12

The Street Carnival

'Mum' or 'mumm'—to go about merry-making in disguise at Christmastide. [—*Webster*]

In the Christmas mummings the chief aim was to surprise by the oddity of the masks, and singularity and splendour of the dresses... but by 6 Edward III [*the year 1333*] the mummers, or masqueraders, were ordered to be whipped out of London. [—*Encyclopedia of Antiquities*, Fosbroke, 1843]

From 1808 to 1859, masquerade and Mumming were eventually outlawed [in Philadelphia] as 'common nuisances.' [*The Philadelphia Mummers*, P.A.Masters, 2007]

STUDENT MUMMER (L.RICHTER, 1844)

1. From those quotes, it sounds like the customs of the traditional Christmas had more in common with the Venice Carnival or with Mardi Gras than with our modern Christmas: that it was a great street party, and people often wore costumes and masks?

—That's about it.

'MASQUERADE IN ST MARK'S PIAZZA, VENICE' (*I.L.N.*, 1864)

2. Did 'mumming' then not necessarily involve any performance—just wandering around in a mask or disguise?

—Apparently no more was necessary. Also, it would seem (from church condemnations as much as from old prints) that Christmas merrymakers had a particular penchant for cross-dressing (men wearing women's clothes and women wearing men's) and for wearing animal masks. The Church particularly disapproved of the custom of women wearing men's clothes, considering that this made women more inclined to 'publick Dancings.'

(*I.L.N.*, 1842)

3. With everyone that fond of putting on costumes, the streets at Christmas, all over Europe, must have presented quite a spectacle.

—Yes, and although publicly going about disguised at Christmas was officially banned for much of the time, people continued to do so.

4. Who banned Mumming?

MUMMERS
(*ILLUSTRATED SPORTING & DRAMATIC NEWS*, 1878)

—The first powerful force to ban it—repeatedly—was the pre-Reformation church, until eventually it decided it was wasting its time. For all the control the church had over its followers, Christians were deaf to decrees forbidding them to go about in funny costumes at Christmas. The pleasure of putting on a mask at that time, and taking to the streets, seems to have outweighed even

Chapter 12

The Street Carnival

the fear of losing one's eternal soul for doing it.

Keeping Christmas Well

5. **What exactly did the church say?**

DANCING MUMMERS IN THE *LUTTRELL PSALTER*, ENGLAND, 1320-40 [*BRITISH LIBRARY*]

—The church specifically blamed the *Kalends* legacy, and the ongoing lure of its traditions (or as the church saw it, the influence of the *Kalends'* pagan gods). For instance, the Council of Trullus decreed in 692 AD:

> ...that the Days called the *Calends* should be intirely stripp'd of their Ceremonies, and the Faithful should no longer observe them: That the publick Dancings of Women should cease, as being the Occasion of much Harm and Ruin, and as being invented and observed in honour of their Gods, and therefore quite averse to the Christian Life. They therefore decreed, that no Man should be Cloathed with a Woman's Garment, no Woman with a Man's. [—Bourne]

6. **But that didn't work?**

GIRLS IN MEN'S CLOTHES (C.H. SHANNON, 1899)

—It had no effect whatever. The cross-dressing tradition remained so popular that one important 19th century authority (who had been Principal Librarian of the British Museum) gives it as the definition of 'mumming':

MAN IN WOMAN'S DRESS

> Mumming is a sport of this festive season

which consists in changing clothes between men and women, who, when dressed in each other's habits, go from one neighbour's house to another, partaking of Christmas cheer and making merry with them in disguise. [—Ellis]

Chapter 12

The Street Carnival

MAN DRESSED AS A WOMAN - THE 'BESSY' - ON PLOUGH MONDAY (THE FIRST MONDAY AFTER JANUARY 6th - THE DAY AGRICULTURAL WORK WAS RESUMED AFTER CHRISTMAS IN MUCH OF ENGLAND)
G. WALKER, 1814

7. Who else banned it?

—England repeatedly did, and its first ban on the practice carried a sanction that ought to have worried revellers. Fosbroke in his *Encyclopedia of Antiquities* (1843) describes both the practice of Mumming and the sanctions introduced against it in the 14th century:

> Those who could not procure masks rubbed their faces with soot, or painted them. In the Christmas mummings the chief aim was to surprise by the oddity of the masks, and singularity and splendour of the dresses. Everything was out of nature and propriety. They were the common holiday amusements of young people of both sexes; but by 6 Edward III [the year 1333] the mummers, or masqueraders, were ordered *to be whipped out of London.*

MUMMERS VISIT (CASSELL, *CHRISTMAS IN THE OLDEN TIME*, 1887, N.Y.)

8. Well that particular sanction must have had an effect?

(E.&G. DALZIEL, 1850)

—Surprisingly, no. The drive to wander around in public at Christmas wearing a costume and mask turned out to be stronger than the fear of being whipped.

The authorities of the City of London tried again, however, in 1418 with the proclamation:

> The mayor and aldermen charge on the king's behalf, and this city, that no …person, of what estate, degree, or condition what ever he be, during this holy time of Christmas, be so hardy in any wise to walk by night in any manner mumming, plays, interludes or any other disguises with any feigned beards, painted visors, deformed or coloured visages in any wise, on pain of imprisonment of their bodies and making fine after the discretion of the mayor and aldermen.

MUMMERS
(*ILLUSTRATED SPORTING & DRAMATIC NEWS*, 1879)

9. So did that work?

—Again, no, but they made another attempt a century later in the reign of Henry VIII with an

order making it an offence—
> to appear abroad like mummers, their faces covered with vizors, and in disguised apparel.

10. I'm guessing that didn't work either?

—No, we know it didn't because later in the century frustrated Puritans were still condemning the Masking and Mumming going on at Christmas.

Chapter 12

The Street Carnival

'MUMMERS AT CHRISTMAS IN THE OLDEN TIME' (CORBOULD, *I.L.N.*, 1866)

11. Am I right in thinking they banned Mumming in parts of America too?

—Yes:
> From 1808 to 1859, masquerade and Mumming were eventually outlawed [in Philadelphia] as 'common nuisances'; in a parallel development, New Orleans officials outlawed the *Mardi Gras* on the grounds that celebrations undermined civic order. Because local constables rarely enforced the ban, the celebrations continued. After city consultation, the practices were tolerated but they occurred under the watchful eyes of professional police.

MUMMER, PHILADELPHIA, 1924

[From *The Philadelphia Mummers: Building Community Through Play*, P. A. Masters, 2007.]

12. What about other places—was it banned anywhere else?

—Almost everywhere it existed, the authorities banned it at one time or another, but never with much success. This is how one text summed it up:

'DUEL AFTER A MASQUERADE' (J-L. GÉRÔME, 1857)

> In the long history of mumming in Great Britain and America, and probably elsewhere, a common pattern is evident, the rowdiness and dangerous (sometimes criminal) nature of the disguised mummers has been met by repeated civic bans on the practice. These bans have a curious habit of repeating themselves in time, suggesting the deep-seated nature of the custom of mumming, which has been suppressed only to rise again in the old or a new form.
> [From *Christmas Mumming in Newfoundland*, G. Stiles, H. Halpert, & G. Story, eds., 1971.]

13. And Mumming still exists both in Newfoundland and in Philadelphia, doesn't it?

PHILADELPHIA MUMMERS PARADE OF 1892

—The custom of Mumming survived (or has been revived) in something like its original form in Newfoundland. In Philadelphia, the determination to go about in disguise was re-directed into a colourful New Year's parade (which remains a great popular event).

14. Re-directed from what? What did Mummers do before that?

—Sometimes they just 'made merry' in their disguises

on the streets and in taverns. But there was also an interesting custom of calling to houses, performing minor plays, or at least acting the part of characters (whose disguises they were wearing) during the visit.

ST STEPHEN'S DAY MUMMERS ('WREN BOYS') CALLING TO A COUNTRY PUB IN IRELAND, C. 1950

Chapter 12

The Street Carnival

15. Was that popular—I mean did people like it when a group in disguise came to their house?

—It depended on the house. The temperament of the householders as much as the behaviour of the mummers seemed to determine whether the visit would be an interesting social interchange or a worrying nuisance. There is a sweet description in a book on Philadelphia Mumming practices of how an 'old Quaker family'—not Christmas-keepers, and whose traditions would have been very far

'THE WREN BOYS' IN CORK CITY (ON ST STEPHEN'S DAY, 26th DECEMBER)

(*DRAWN:* D. MACLISE C. 1840, *ENGR:* LANDELLS, 1841)

'HUNTING THE WREN':

ONE OF THE MORE MYSTERIOUS CHRISTMAS CUSTOMS, 'HUNTING THE WREN' ON ST STEPHEN'S DAY, SURVIVED IN IRELAND (FROWNED ON BY THE CATHOLIC CHURCH) TO THE 20th CENTURY [*PHOTOS ABOVE & FOLLOWING*]. ORIGINALLY, THE CUSTOM INVOLVED KILLING LIVE WRENS, AND 'WREN BOYS' (OFTEN IN COSTUMES MADE OF STRAW) WOULD BEAR THE TINY CORPSES—ATTACHED TO HOLLY BUSHES— FROM HOUSE TO HOUSE SEEKING MONEY 'TO BURY THE WREN.' IN MORE MODERN TIMES—ESPECIALLY SINCE THE REVIVAL OF THE CUSTOM IN CERTAIN AREAS IN THE LAST FEW DECADES (TO RAISE MONEY FOR CHARITY)—A FAKE WREN (OR NO WREN AT ALL) IS USED.

Keeping Christmas Well

removed from holiday mumming—believed that their masked visitors should be received:

ARRIVAL OF MUMMERS (*THE BOOK OF CHRISTMAS*, R. SEYMOUR, 1836)

It was considered the proper thing... to give the leading mummer a few pence of dole, which in the language of the present time, they would 'pool' and buy cakes and beer. It was also regarded as the right thing to do to invite them into the house and [give them] mulled cider...and homemade cakes. It was considered a great breach of decorum and of etiquette to address or otherwise recognize the mummer by any name other than the name of the character he was assuming. [—Masters, 2007.]

16. So for most of the history of Christmas, there was no question of celebrating the holiday as a low-key, private, family affair?

—None whatsoever. The convention that everyone was equal at Christmas influenced everything. The general principle that the most destitute could go around the streets in masks claiming equality with the rich

ABOVE: CHRISTMAS MORNING MASQUERADER, TURKS & CAICOS ISLANDS, 21st CENT. (PHOTO: DAVID BOWEN, T.C.I. COMMISSION)

MUMMERS, IRELAND, MID-20th CENTURY

in their mansions often caused unease within those mansions. The poor however cherished and developed the tradition of equality, which caused some Christmas customs to be modified over time, and an element of beggary or social blackmail to enter into them.

17. In what way?

—In England, for instance, there was a strong 26th December (Boxing Day) tradition of giving money (not always willingly) to servants, tradesmen, etc. Thomas Hervey wrote in 1836:

'BOXING DAY' (G. CRUIKSHANK, 1836)

Chapter 12

The Street Carnival

> Most of our readers know that it was the practice...for families to keep lists of the servants, of tradesmen and others, who were considered to have a claim upon them for a Christmas-box, at this time. The practice, besides opening a door to great extortion, is...of considerable annoyance, and is on the decline. There is, however, as they who are exposed to it know, some danger in setting it at defiance, where it is yet in force. ... Boxing-day...is still a great day in London, ...every street resounds with the clang of hall-door knockers. Rap follows rap in *rap*id succession...

AN EARTHEN-WARE CHRISTMAS BOX (*ENGR.* W.B.SCOTT, 1850)

'BOXING DAY' (*THE BOOK OF CHRISTMAS*, R. SEYMOUR, 1836)

Keeping Christmas Well

18. So money was given out on 26th December less out of goodwill than because it was too risky not to do so?

—So it seems. Pepys, for instance wrote in his Diary (1668) of having been 'called up by drums and trumpets... boxes have cost me much money this Christmas, and will do more.' These words were echoed by Hervey's London Publisher (W. Spooner) who made the following entry in his journal on Boxing Day 1834:

Called out by the parish beadle, dustmen, and charity boys. The postman, street-sweepers, chimney-sweepers,

'BOXING DAY CALLERS' (*THE GRAPHIC*, 1881)

lamp-lighters, ...will all be sure to wait upon me. These fellows have cost me much money this Christmas, and will do more the next.

18. I see.

—Also, in the British Isles, the Wassail Bowl evolved, over centuries of Christmasses, from being an accessory of the rich, used for their celebrations, to a device put into service by the poor for collecting money at Christmas.

'WASSAIL' (*I.L.N.*, 1856)

19. What does 'Wassail' mean anyway?

—The word 'wassail' comes from the Middle English *'wæs hæil!'* and means 'be well!' Wassail traditions involved a hot drink, a large bowl and various customs, in particular a toast to someone's health. The bowl itself was often made of wood (lignum vitae) or silver or pewter; and the drink that went into it traditionally included roasted apples, which would burst, and give the drink a distinctive appearance that in turn

Chapter 12

The Street Carnival

'WASSAIL.'
(SEYMOUR, 1836)

would give the classic wassail drink its name *'lamb's wool.'* Sometimes pieces of toast were floated on top, and this is thought to be the origin of the use of the word 'toast' for wishing someone well.

20. So just to be clear, what are the directions for making a wassail drink?

WASSAIL BOWL (*RECOLLECTIONS OF OLD CHRISTMAS*, 1850)

—Well, here are two 19th century recommendations:

It is a good-natured bowl, and accommodates itself to the means of all classes, rich and poor. You may have it of the costliest wine or the humblest malt liquor. But in no case must the roasted apples be forgotten. They are the *sine qua non* of the wassail-bowl, as the wassail bowl is of the day (in this case New Year's Day); and very pleasant they are, provided they are not mixed up too much with the beverage, balmy, comfortable, and different, a sort of meat in the drink, but innocent withal and reminding you of the orchards. They mix their flavour with the beverage, and the beverage with them. [—*Leigh Hunt's London Journal*, 1834]

It should be composed, by those who can afford it, of some rich wine, highly spiced and sweetened, with roasted apples floating on its surface. But ale was more commonly substituted for the wine, mingled with nutmeg, ginger, sugar, toast, and roasted crabs (crab-apples). [—Hervey, 1836]

21. So did the wassail start as an English tradition—not an adaptation of a classical tradition?

WASSAIL (BROCK, 1905)

—That's right. In the royal court and the manors of medieval England, the wassail bowl was used (sometimes with elaborate conventions) for making toasts.

22. And among the less wealthy?

—Numerous traditions developed.

'To go wassailing' often meant carrying a bowl of a drink called 'lamb's wool' … from house to house, singing carols, and expecting some gratuity. [—*Webster*]

(ENGRAVING: VIZETELLY, 1851)

Usually it was women who carried the bowl, and there were special wassail songs.

23. And that was a popular custom?

—It might have been more popular with

wassailers than with householders. Some people did not like being asked for money. John Selden, for instance, a sixteenth-century writer, wrote in *Table Talk*:

>...as wenches do by their wassails at New Year's tide, they present you with a cup, and you must drink of a slabby stuff; but the meaning is, you must give them moneys ten times more than it is worth.

WOMEN WASSAILING (J. GILBERT, 1896)

24. Was there a special night for this?

—The most popular times were Christmas Eve, New Year's Eve and, in particular, Twelfth Night.

25. Any other Wassail customs?

—There was a strong tradition of bringing the wassail bowl to orchards (particularly on Twelfth Night).

WASSAILING APPLE TREES, DEVON (*I.L.N.*, 1861)

The purpose was to ensure a good apple crop for the year. The drink would be sprinkled on apple trees, and their health drunk to.

26. Were there other Christmas customs that evolved over time as they were taken up by the poor?

—Have you heard of 'Waits'?

'WAITS'
(CALDECOTT, 1886)

Keeping Christmas Well

27. I've seen the word on old engravings. They seem like they were just groups performing Christmas carols on the streets, often for people who didn't want to hear them, and looking pretty raggedy.

—Eventually, that's more or less what the term 'wait' came to mean.—

> WAIT: one of a group who serenade for gratuities, esp. at the Christmas season. [—*Webster*]

'WAITS' (*THE ILLUSTRATED SPORTING & DRAMATIC NEWS*, 1890)

Originally, however, 'Waits' were something quite different—a colourful phenomenon with an

'WAITS AT 3.00 AM' (R. SEYMOUR, *BOOK OF CHRISTMAS*, 1836)

interesting mix of duties that is now hard to believe. 'Town Waits' were musicians—very accomplished musicians, expected to compose and play music for civic functions etc.—but also a town Watch. They were municipal employees, required to patrol with their instruments at night, and keep the city streets safe. (The name 'Waits' was British, but Continental cities had the equivalent under different names). They also had an alarm-clock function—an obligation to wake people in the morning with their music.

Chapter 12

The Street Carnival

WAITS, LEICESTER 1700S (HENRY STEER, C.1900)

STADTPFEIFER, NÜRNBERG 1519

WAITS IN BRITTANY - '*SONNEURS*' (*I.L.N.*, 1853)

'A SAD RECITAL' - FRENCH WAITS (J. DENNEULIN 1875)

28. You're serious?

—Yes. Over time, it appears that their function as official musicians (including as singers) increased and their function as watchmen decreased, but did not disappear entirely. In 1620, Waits were dismissed in Manchester for—

17th CENTURY WAITS

> ...failing to perform their duties which they ought to do in the winter season, by their walking and going abroad in the night whereby they might discover many dangers and misdemeanours which may happen to fall out in a night. [From *Medieval and Renaissance Drama in England* vol.7, by Leeds Barroll, 1995.]

29. Do they still exist in England?

—They were made redundant by the *Municipal Corporations Act* of 1835.

30. That's a pity. What did they do then?

—When they no longer had an official job, the redundant Waits did the best they could with their abilities. They continued to play, particularly in the weeks before Christmas, seeking tips (or even food and drink) for their efforts.

'LONDON WAITS' (*I.L.N.*, 1848)

31. That made sense.

—Yes, although the music late at night was not always welcome. This wonderfully succinct description of what Waits actually did, and how much (or little) they were appreciated was given by London footman William Tayler on 26th December 1837:

Chapter 12

The Street Carnival

CHRISTMAS WAITS, LONDON (*I.L.N.* 1853)

These are a set of men that goe about the streets playing musick in the night after people are in bed and a-sleepe. Some people are very fond of hearing them, but for my own part, I don't admire being aroused from a sound sleep by a whole band of musick and perhaps not get to sleep again for an houre or two. [*Diary of Wm. Tayler (& waits website)*]

32. O.K.

—The street musicians fell even further in public esteem when amateur groups, with no musical ability, also began to perform on the streets looking for money. The same term 'Waits' was applied equally to all of them (and ultimately came to be applied to every group of carollers or musicians at Christmas, children or adults). Sometimes there was an element of blackmail in the

COUNTRY CAROL SINGERS (R.SEYMOUR, 1836)

performances—for money, the musicians would agree *not* to return and wake a household in the middle of the night.

33. I see.

(E. & G. DALZIEL, *CHRISTMAS COMES BUT ONCE A YEAR*, 1850)

—All the same, the part the tuneless street-singers played in preserving the carol appears to have been significant (although, even at Christmas, the singers were more likely to render non-seasonal ballads, or music popularized by the barrel organ, than Christmas tunes). As well as performing, they also sold cheap carol sheets, and it was these sheets in particular that helped save the carol from extinction.

Indeed, many carols are yet printed in

LONDON CAROL SINGERS SELLING CAROL SHEETS (*ILN.*, 1847)

London for the chapmen, or dealers in cheap literature; some scores of half-penny and penny carols of this description ... and single or broadside pieces. Several of these carols have wood-cuts of the rudest description; others again, have embellishments that might have been considered very creditable for the price

Chapter 12

The Street Carnival

at which they are afforded ... Some of these carols, I was informed by the publishers, are in considerable request, and are printed off as the demand requires. [—Sandys, 1833]

LONDON CAROL SINGERS SELLING CAROL SHEETS (R.SEYMOUR, 1836)

34. So in fact the singers did posterity a great service?

—They may have done, but their contemporaries did not much appreciate their efforts:

It is said that the lion will turn and flee from a maid in the pride of her purity. We would rather meet him under the protection of a group of London carol-singers. We would undertake to explore the entire of central Africa, well provisioned, and in such company, without the slightest apprehension, excepting such as was suggested by the music itself.
[—Hervey, 1836]

'RIVAL WAITS' (A. FORESTER, 1896)

CHAPTER 13

Other Days & Seasons around Christmas

Saint Martin's Day—11th November
(St Martin of Tours, buried 11th November 397)

1. Isn't it on St Martin's Day that you eat goose and drink wine in Germany and Austria?

—Yes, or as a disapproving English text of 1841 put it:

CEILING: ST MARTIN'S CHURCH, ZILLIS (SWITZERLAND) C. 1110 AD

> The Feast of St Martin is a day of debauch among Christians on the Continent. The new wines are then to be tasted, and the Saint's day is celebrated with carousing. [—Ellis]

2. Who was Saint Martin?

The story is that he was a Roman soldier who converted to Christianity. The most famous legend about him is that, while still a soldier, he cut his cloak in two to give part of it to a beggar, and then had a vision of Jesus wearing the half-cloak. He converted, and became Bishop of Tours in 371 AD.

ST MARTIN OF TOURS FRESCO, ASSISI (S. MARTINI C. 1318)

3. How did the tradition arise of eating and drinking so much on that day?

—St Perpetuus may be responsible for that. In about the year 480 AD, he decreed a fast three times a week from 11th November to Christmas (a period often called '40 days,' but really 43 days). The day before the fasting began—St Martin's Day—became one of heavy eating and drinking. This long period of Advent was later shortened to about four weeks, and the requirement to fast was ended, but the tradition of feasting on 11th November remained.

4. Why is goose the traditional food?

—Take your pick of the legends. One (which is funny, but makes no sense as the inspiration for a goose-eating custom) is that St Martin was preaching in a village, and was interrupted repeatedly by a honking goose. He ordered the goose to be killed. Afterwards it was cooked and served to him, and he choked to death eating it. Another is that he tried to hide once in a goose house to avoid discovery by those coming to tell him he had been given the job of bishop—a job he did not want, as he wished to lead the life of a hermit. The geese, however, revealed his hiding place by making noise. Hence a reason for putting geese in the oven or in the pot on that day.

'THE GOOSE MERCHANT' (*I.L.N.*, 1886)

MARTINMAS GOOSE FAIR (*I.L.N.*, 1873)

Chapter 13

Other Days & Seasons around Christmas

Saint Lucia's Day—13th December

Keeping Christmas Well

5. Is Saint Lucia's Day a Swedish holiday?

—Yes, it's a big holiday there and the start of Christmas, but is also celebrated in other Scandinavian countries as well as in parts of Italy, Malta, Swedish-influenced parts of the U.S., etc.

6. Who was St Lucia?

SAINT LUCIA (HOLDING A PAIR OF EYES; D. BECCAFUMI, 1521, SIENA)

—She was a fourth-century Christian martyr from Sicily.

7. Why is it that, on that day, girls in Sweden wear candles on their heads?

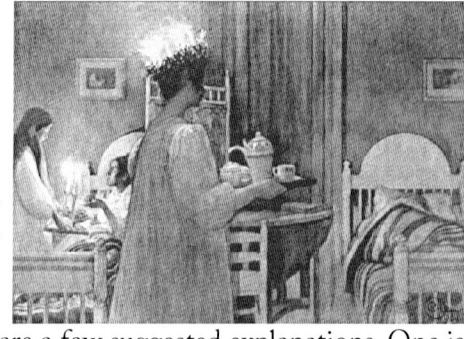

'LUCIA MORNING' (C. LARSSON, SWEDEN, 1908)

—There are a few suggested explanations. One is that Lucia was said to have secretly fed Christians hiding in the catacombs, and wore candles on her head so that her hands would be free for carrying food. Another is that December 13th was the winter solstice in the old Julian Calendar and the candles are a remnant of a Scandinavian pagan festival of light. Also it may be relevant that Lucia's eyes (which she is often depicted holding) were said to have been gouged out, either by her own hands, or by the hands of her persecutors.

SAINT STEPHEN'S DAY—26th DECEMBER

8. Who was Saint Stephen?

—St Stephen was the first Christian martyr. He was stoned to death about the year 35 AD. *The Stoning of Saint Stephen [>]* was the first painting of the Dutch artist, Rembrandt (done in 1625 when he was aged 19). The saint's name is popularly best known because his feast day is mentioned in the carol, *Good King Wenceslas* (lyrics by J. M. Neale) published in 1853.

(DETAIL - REMBRANDT, 1625)

Chapter 13

Other Days & Seasons around Christmas

< CHRISTMAS CAROLS
OLD AND NEW
(F.A. FRASER, 1871)

SAINT JOHN'S DAY—27th DECEMBER
(ST JOHN THE EVANGELIST, DIED C.99 AD)

9. What about St John's Day, December 27th?

—This day is interesting because of its wine customs (in memory of St John who is said to have been unharmed by a cup of poisoned wine after he had blessed it with the Sign of the Cross).

ST JOHN THE EVANGELIST
(EL GRECO C. 1600, PRADO)

A quantity of wine is brought to church to be blessed by the priest after Mass, and is taken away by the people to be drunk at home. There are many popular beliefs about the magical powers of this wine... in Bavaria some is kept for use as a medicine in sickness. In Styria (Austria)… on this day even babes in the cradle are made to join in the family drinking.   [—Miles]

FEEDING BLESSED WINE (OF ST JOHN) TO A SICK CHILD

CHILDERMAS—28th DECEMBER
(HOLY INNOCENTS' DAY)

10. What about December 28th, Holy Innocents' Day or 'Childermas'?

—Childermas is interesting because of some truly terrible old Continental-European customs associated with it. It is said to be the day King Herod killed all the boys in Bethlehem who were two years old or under; and in some countries on that day, children were whipped in memory of the event. In general, it is held to be an extremely unlucky day: Louis XI of France would never do any business on that day, and Edward IV of England postponed his coronation because it was fixed for that day.

In Ireland, it was called 'the Cross Day of the year,' and it was said that anything then begun must have an unlucky ending. [—Miles]

'MASSACRE OF THE INNOCENTS' (RUBENS, 1611)

Seasons Before Christmas: Novena of Christmas

Chapter 13

Other Days & Seasons around Christmas

11. What's the 'Novena' of Christmas?

—Many people have never heard of the Novena of Christmas. Others say (often mystifying their listeners) that they regard Christmas as beginning on 16th December. This is the Novena of Christmas. It amounts to nine days of preparation for Christmas.

PREPARING FOR CHRISTMAS - 'THE WOOD-GATHERERS' (L.RICHTER, DRESDEN, 1858)

12. Is a 'Novena' similar to an 'Octave'?

—Not exactly.
A Novena is a nine days' private or public devotion... to obtain special graces. The Octave (as the eight days following Christmas and the Epiphany*) has more of a festal character; to the Novena belongs that of hopeful mourning, of yearning, of prayer. [Summarized from *The Catholic Encyclopedia*.]   (*—*Before Vatican II*)

Again, it was a date to which more attention was paid in the past than at present. For instance, schools in 18th century Williamsburg, Virginia, closed for Christmas on 16th December.

Omne bene
Sine poena
Tempus est ludendi;
Venit hora
Absque mora
Libros deponendi.

Old School Holiday Song.

Seasons Before Christmas: Advent

13. So when exactly does Advent start and finish now?

—Since the sixth century, the season of Advent starts on the Sunday nearest to November 30th (either before or after). The earliest it can begin is November 27th and the latest is December 3rd. It includes the four Sundays before Christmas.

In the Catholic, Anglican and Lutheran churches, Advent is the regarded as the start of the liturgical year.

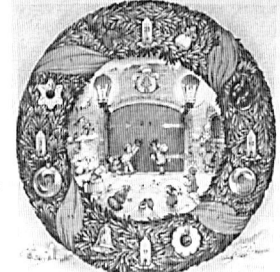
ADVENT CALENDAR, LEIPZIG

14. Does Advent have a purpose?

—It is a season of waiting for Christmas and preparing for Christmas. It used to be a penitential season, marked by fasting and the prohibition of dancing, public recreations and marriage festivities, but now it is regarded more as a season of hope.

15. Are there traditions of Advent?

—There's the Advent wreath, of course, and for children, the Advent calendar.

16. Is the Advent calendar a very old tradition?

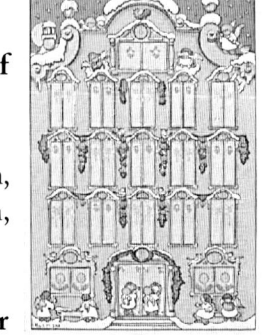
ADVENT CALENDAR WITH 19 DOORS (6th–24th DECEMBER), MUNICH, C. 1930

—Apparently not. A handmade calendar was

produced in Germany in 1851. Printed calendars (shortly to have little doors, varying in number from 19 to 32) appeared in the early 20th century, and finally (possibly in the 1950s) the wonderful calendars with chocolates behind the doors.

17. What exactly is an Advent wreath?

—Let me pass you over to Maria von Trapp. In the chapter 'An Austrian Christmas' from her autobiography, *The Story of the Trapp Family Singers*, published in 1949, she gives a fascinating, intimate account of a very thoroughly-kept Advent in pre-World-War-II Austria.

Chapter 13

Other Days & Seasons around Christmas

VON TRAPP FAMILY (1940S)

Then an aspirant nun (a candidate for the novitiate at the 8th century Benedictine Abbey of Nonnberg—'a place of unearthly beauty' as she put it) and deeply conscious of the religious significance of Advent, she describes her first Christmas in the von Trapp household, as a teacher to one of the children:

'Where do you usually put up the Advent wreath?' [she asks her pupil, also named Maria]

'Put up what?'

I was aghast. 'Don't you have an Advent wreath every year?'

'No, never. What is it?'

'It is a large wreath made of fir greens, holding four candles, one for each of the four Sundays of Advent. People put it up in their living-rooms. It reminds

BENEDICTINE NUNS' CHOIR

PROCESSIONAL OF NONNBERG ABBEY SALZBURG, C. 1510

them of the coming of Christmas. They light the candles and sing Advent songs...'

ADVENT WREATH (AUSTRIA)

Maria then describes making an Advent wreath—winding fir twigs around an old buggy wheel, securing them with thread, putting four spikes through the wheel to hold four candles, and then putting four long pieces of ribbon around the wreath to suspend it from the ceiling.

On the first Sunday of Advent, one candle is lit. (On the following Sundays of Advent, two candles, then three candles, and finally all four candles are lit). Also on the first Sunday of Advent, she describes how 'all the small and big children of Austria' write a letter to the Christ Child who 'is believed to come down from heaven, Himself personally, on Christmas Eve, accompanied by angels and bring the Christmas tree and the wonderful things under it. ...'

She describes how the Christ Child was just one of the gift-givers

'CHRISTMAS EVE ANGEL' (GUSTAVE DORÉ, PARIS C. 1880)

who would visit Austrian children at Christmas time, the other, of course, being St Nicholas:

> The excitement of the first Sunday in Advent had hardly died down when the sixth of December came around, one of the most momentous days for all houses where children lived. On the vigil of this day Saint Nikolaus comes down to earth to visit all the little ones.

THE CHRIST-CHILD AND ANGELS BRING THE CHRISTMAS TREE AND
CHILDREN'S PRESENTS (L. RICHTER, GERMANY, 1855)

Chapter 13

Other Days & Seasons around Christmas

The kind Saint Nicholas is followed, however,—
by the Krampus, an ugly, black little devil with a
long, red tongue, a pair of horns, and a long tail

VISIT OF NIKOLAUS & THE KRAMPUS (FZ. PAUMGARRTEN C. 1825, AUSTRIA)

Keeping Christmas Well

so the visit might work out well or badly. Good children get presents, bad children might get left a switch.

The Christmas tree was decorated just before Christmas Eve, and kept concealed from the children until the night of Christmas Eve, when the drawing-room doors were dramatically thrown open to reveal it in its glory—hung with sweets and fruits, and lit by one hundred and twenty wax candles.

ABOVE: 'KNECHT RUPRECHT' (THE GERMAN *KRAMPUS*) MAKES HIS INQUIRIES (L. RICHTER, 1852)

ABOVE: 'CHRISTMAS TIME,' (H. STUBENRAUCH, GERMANY, 1900)

'ROUND THE CHRISTMAS TREE' (V. JOHANSEN, DENMARK, 1891)

—All of that, and the Twelve Days of Christmas had not even started. Now, that's keeping Christmas well!

Chapter 14
—Afters: a Miscellany—

1: Notes on Four
Traditional Christmas Dishes

 (i) The Plum Pudding

The Plum Pudding: a boiled or steamed pudding of flour or breadcrumbs, raisins, currants and other fruits, suet, eggs, and spices and other flavouring matters. [—*Webster*]

Plum pudding 'is a truly national dish,' wrote English writer Thomas K. Hervey in 1836, 'and refuses to flourish out of England. It can obtain no footing in France. A Frenchman will dress like an Englishman, swear like an Englishman, and get drunk like an Englishman; but if you would offend him forever, compel him to eat plum pudding.' [—*The Book of Christmas*, 1836]

Whatever about its taste (or its weight as the finish of a heavy meal), the plum pudding *looks* great. Round, flying a sprig of holly, and often in flames, it is loved by illustrators, 'The Crown of the Feast'

WAITER IN A FRENCH HOTEL STRUGGLES WITH PLUM PUDDING (CLEAVER, *THE GRAPHIC* 1909)

'THE CROWN OF THE FEAST' (E.M. WARD, *I.L.N.*, 1868)

Keeping Christmas Well

is the title of one such illustration, and that usually is the status given to it by artists. An exception of 1906 [right >] depicts a dog's horrified reaction to an offer of plum pudding. At sea, the plum pudding had a special status:

'PUDDING IN PERIL...ON A WARSHIP' (*WAR ILLUSTRATED*, 1916)

If the Christmas pudding is proverbial among soldiers and civilians as a symbol of the festive season, in the Fleet it is something of a rite, and no sailor-cook would dare to face the ship's company after having omitted it from the Christmas menu. Furthermore...it is certain not to be entrusted to anyone...not absolutely assured of his sea-legs. [—*War Illustrated*, 1916]

ABOVE: 'STEADY BOYS STEADY - PLUM PUDDING AT SEA' (*THE GRAPHIC*, 1875)

BELOW: 'THE POOR ACTRESS'S CHRISTMAS DINNER' (R.B. MARTINEAU, 1826-1869, *ASHMOLEAN MUSEUM, OXFORD*)

∧ *LEFT:* 'ENTRY OF THE CHRISTMAS PUDDING - QUEEN'S DINNER TO WIDOWS & ORPHANS OF THOSE WHO FELL IN THE [BOER] WAR' (*THE GRAPHIC*, 1903)

(ii) Boar's Head

Chapter 14

Afters

A Christmas Miscellany

Boar's Head was another favourite of illustrators. A dish probably of continental origin (possibly from Scandinavia) and popular throughout much of Europe. In England, the Boar's Head (often weighing about 70 lb) was presented with much ceremony at Christmas banquets, to the singing of a boar's head carol. The tradition never fully recovered after the Puritan era, but there is still a Boar's Head dinner at Queen's College, Oxford, [<] on Christmas Day.

'BRINGING IN THE BOAR'S HEAD' (J. GILBERT, *I.L.N.*, 1855)

To prepare the dish, cooks bone the head, leaving in place the jawbones and tusks. A stuffing (the recipes varying with the cooks) is then prepared.

'BRINGING IN THE BOAR'S HEAD AT QUEEN'S COLLEGE OXFORD' (*I.L.N.*, 1846)

A 1934 cookbook by Viconte de Mauduit included this tempting Boar's Head recipe from Brittany with two stuffings: one of minced pig's liver, apples, onions, sage and rosemary, which is arranged 'all around the inside of the head about half-an-inch in thickness. Then a second stuffing of 'sausage meat, squares of ox tongue, chopped truffles, chopped apples, chopped mushrooms, chopped pistachio nuts and minced rosemary' fills the remainder of the space: '…add one wineglass of Calvados (or sherry) and an equal quantity of cream.'…The boar's ears, which have been cut off and boiled separately, are replaced on the head with a skewer. 'Place the head on an oblong dish, surround it with slices of truffles, slices of apples, and strew with rosemary.' [—*The Vicomte In The Kitchen*, Vicomte de Mauduit, Covici-Friede Publishers, New York, 1934]

PREPARING (1878 *ABOVE*) AND PRESENTING (1871 *BELOW*) THE BOAR'S HEAD (H.S.MARKS, *I.L.N.*)

(iii) Brawn

Chapter 14

Afters

A Christmas Miscellany

This meat is referred to casually in old texts about Christmas, but was not, it seems, the modern 'brawn' (a product, sometimes called 'head cheese,' made largely from the head-meat of a domestic pig or wild boar), but the flesh of a boar prepared in a particular way. Here are two early 19th century explanations of 'brawn':

'UN SOLITAIRE' ['A ROGUE BOAR'] (A.SPECHT, *L'ILLUSTRATION*, 1903)

From 1807—

BRAWN: The flesh of a boar when souced or pickled; for which end the boar should be old; because the older he is, the more horny will the brawn be. The method of preparing brawn is as

'A BOAR HUNT' (P. MᴬᶜQUOID, 1884)

follows: The boar being killed, it is the fliches only, without the legs, that are made brawn; the bones of which are to be taken out, and then the flesh sprinkled with salt, and laid in a tray, that the blood may drain off: Then it is to be salted a little, and rolled up as hard as possible. The length of the collar of brawn should be as much as one side of the boar will bear, so that when rolled up it will be nine or ten inches diameter. The collar thus rolled up, is boiled in a copper, or large kettle, till it is so tender, that a straw can be run through it. Then it is set aside, till it is thoroughly cold, and put it into the following pickle: To every gallon of water, put a handful or two of salt, and as much wheat-bran: Boil them together, then drain the bran as clear as you can from the liquor; and when the liquor is quite cold put the brawn into it. [—*The New Encyclopædia, or Universal Dictionary of Arts and Sciences, including the whole of Dr. Johnson's Dictionary of the English Language*, London, 1807.]

'WILD BOARS IN THE SNOW' (*L'ILLUSTRATION*, 1863)

And a different explanation of brawn from 1836—
BRAWN: It is manufactured from the flesh of large boars, which are suffered to live in a half-wild state, and, when put up to fatten, are strapped and belted tight round the principal parts of the carcass, in order to make the flesh become dense and brawny. This article comes to market in rolls about two feet long and ten inches in diameter, packed in wicker baskets. [—Thomas K. Hervey, *The Book of Christmas*, London, 1836]

And a COLLAR OF BRAWN—
When the roll of brawn was wrapped tightly in linen, a COLLAR OF BRAWN was defined as: *the quantity bound up in one parcel* [—*A Dictionary of the English Language*, Samuel Johnson, 1766 ed.]

(iv) The Turkey

Called the Great American Bird, the turkey is a native of the Western Hemisphere and as early as the 16th century was domesticated in Mexico. [—*James Beard's American Cookery*, 1972]

Also in the 16th century, the turkey came to Europe, brought first from Mexico by the Spanish Conquistadores. It was popularized in France by the Jesuits, where it is still sometimes called *jésuite* (its more usual French name *dinde* coming from *poule d'Indes :* 'Indian chicken,' from the time when Mexico was thought to be in the Indies). [–*Larousse Gastronomique*]

(W.WEEKES, *I.L.N.*, 1888)

A trader called William Strickland is believed to have brought the turkey to England, being said to have sold six wild turkeys in Bristol in 1526. He later made a fortune as a turkey importer.

The turkey quickly became popular on the Continent:

In Spain, it was customary for patients

'BUYING THE CHRISTMAS TURKEY AT MALAGA MARKET IN SPAIN' (E.BUCKMAN, *THE GRAPHIC*, 1890)

to send their medical attendants presents of turkeys, so that doctors in large practices had to open a kind of trade in them. [—Sandys]

In England, however, few farmers would rear turkeys, regarding them as delicate and unprofitable, likely to die as chicks. As a result, the turkey remained rare and expensive there until the 20th century, although much-appreciated by the few who could afford it as a better-tasting and easier-to-cook bird than traditional great festal birds such as the swan or the peacock. For the majority in England, the goose (or the capon) remained the traditional Christmas bird:

'DINDES DE NOËL À LONDRES' ['CHRISTMAS TURKEYS IN LONDON'] (L'ILLUSTRATION, FRANCE 1904)

> Turkies and geese are... common at Christmas, the latter being the dish in the western counties, while the turkey prevails in London. [—Sandys, 1833]

DRIVING CHRISTMAS TURKEYS (THE GRAPHIC, 1875)

Most English turkeys were raised in Norfolk for the London market, to which many of them had to travel on foot—a journey that could take two months (the birds first having been walked over a layer of soft tar, so that their

'THE NORFOLK COACH AT CHRISTMAS' (R.SEYMOUR, 1836)

Chapter 14

Afters

A Christmas Miscellany

feet would have a protective covering).

Mrs Beeton wrote of English turkeys in 1861:
—These are reared in great numbers in Suffolk, Norfolk, and several other counties, whence they were wont to be driven to the London market in flocks of several hundreds… Their drivers used to manage them with great facility, by means of a bit of red rag tied to the end of a long stick, which, from the antipathy these birds have to that colour, effectually answered the purpose of a scourge. [—*Book of Household Management*]

Before the railways, other turkeys travelled by coach, and during the Christmas season [according to Hervey, 1836], humans were likely to be refused a place inside the Norfolk-London coach in favour of turkeys, which paid better.

'TOO LATE FOR THE COACH' (R.SEYMOUR, *THE BOOK OF CHRISTMAS*, 1836)

2: The Christmas Cookie

Cookie -vˢ- Biscuit

Cookie (or Cooky) is a North American term for what is called a biscuit in the rest of the English-speaking world. In Scotland, a cookie is a plain bun. In the US and Canada, a biscuit is a quick bread. Forced to choose between the two terms, we are using 'cookie' here because we think it causes less confusion. Also, if you put the adjective Christmas in front of the two words, 'Christmas cookie' communicates something instantly in a way 'Christmas biscuit' cannot quite manage.

'ARRIVAL OF CHRISTMAS COOKIES' (*THE GRAPHIC*, 1890)

At Christmas some years ago, the author of this book stayed at a hotel in Vienna. On Christmas Eve night, the hotel left a plate of Christmas cookies in the bedroom. They were particularly good ones—freshly baked, delicate, and they tasted of Christmas.

To reproduce the exquisite taste of those cookies is not easy. The world is full of wonderful cookbooks with thousands of biscuit/cookie recipes, and working one's way through them is one of the great pleasures of life. Baking cookies is a job that non-cooks can do as successfully as good cooks—it is literally child's play.

The problem is that the end-product of most recipes is often not as good as you expect. Some are bland, some are disappointing in texture, many are very sweet.

(RICHTER, 1858)

Four Easy Cookies

This is a short list of four cookies, which have an arrestingly good taste even to a jaded adult palate. They could not be easier to make, but keep a close eye on them while they are baking. There is no margin for error in the timing of cookie baking: one minute too long, and your tray or trays of a few dozen cookies/biscuits can be ruined.

A reliable oven is your best friend, and it is best to bake a test cookie, or at least a very small initial batch.

In all these recipes, use good butter. Do not even consider using margarine, and make sure the butter has not been hanging around too long, and that it very fresh. For practical reasons, all of the test cookies were made using ordinary, salted butter (and the result was great). This was done because the unsalted butter available locally had been in the shop for a long time and was best avoided. [This is a real risk with unsalted butter. Depending on local taste where you live, the turnover in it might be slow, and you might end up with a pack of butter that is not the freshest—even rancid. It has happened to the writer—be careful.]

Also be careful of your flour. Make sure that is fresh too. This is not a problem for frequent/experienced bakers because (a) they will have

'CHRISTMAS PREPARATIONS,'
(F. GRAVIER, *I.L.N.*, 1886)

Chapter 14

Afters

A Christmas Miscellany

a high turnover of flour, so freshness probably will not be a problem, and (b) they will know flour is supposed to be used quickly. But occasional or Christmas bakers need to be careful. Do not use the bag that has been sitting in your cupboard since last year. Go out and buy a new bag.

'DECEMBER' (*CALENDAR*, 1780)

In fact, freshness is key in relation to all the ingredients, and can be a big issue for the once-a-year baker. Eggs, of course, should be fresh, but so should chocolate. Look at the expiry date on the chocolate, don't use it if it is past that date, and make sure it has not been stored in a hot place or near anything that would taint it. Look obsessively at the expiry date and storage conditions of nuts (and buy organic if possible).

(i) A Grown-up, Chocolate-filled Cookie

The contrast between the slight bitterness of the chocolate and the (relative) sweetness of the dough gives a remarkably good taste. Don't use milk chocolate—the cookie would lack drama.

What is very important in this cookie is the quality of the chocolate (approx. 70% cocoa solids). The proportion of chocolate to biscuit is high, so pick the best-tasting chocolate you can find. (All 70%-72% bars don't taste the same.) A standard 100 gm bar fills about 20 biscuits.

Chapter 14
Afters

A Christmas Miscellany

INGREDIENTS:

114 grams butter,
80 grams sifted confectioner's sugar,
1 tablespoon vanilla extract (not essence)—
   Madagascar is good, do not under-measure;
140 grams approx.* all-purpose flour,
Good dark chocolate (70% approx.) for filling.

[* Dry or damp storage conditions affect the weight of flour. Less flour produces a tastier biscuit—crisper and more buttery; but too little flour may result in a spreading biscuit that does not effectively contain the chocolate filling. For this recipe a test biscuit is particularly useful.]

'BAKER'S ACCIDENT DELIVERING CHRISTMAS STOLLEN' (R.GRÜTZNER, GERMANY, 1882)

Pre-heat oven to 175° Centigrade (350° Fahrenheit).

Break or cut chocolate so that 5 grams can be used in each cookie (usually this involves stacking two smaller pieces).

Combine butter, sugar and vanilla. Blend flour by hand into other ingredients. If necessary, adjust texture of dough with small amount of cream, or flour, as appropriate.

Take approx. 1 level tablespoon of dough and wrap this around the chocolate. Place on un-greased baking sheet. Leave 1" (25 mm) between cookies.

Bake 13 to 15 minutes. Don't let the cookies brown, but ensure they are not under-baked. (Do bake that test cookie).
—Makes 20–24 cookies.

For Christmas, we have decorated these by dropping (carefully) some melted chocolate on top (the same chocolate as the filling) and topping this with edible gold balls.

(RICHTER, 1858)

Keeping Christmas Well

CHOCOLATE-FILLED COOKIES

BUTTERSCOTCH SHORTBREAD COOKIES

(ii) Butterscotch Shortbread

In this butterscotch shortbread cookie, the taste and texture of the sugar are important. A medium brown sugar (not a pale demerara, not a dark muscovado) works best. In testing, we made one batch with a pale demerara and one with a medium demerara. The medium demerara made much the better cookie—candy-like and with a strong butterscotch flavour. If you are lucky in the taste of your sugar, this can be the best-tasting cookie ever.

Chapter 14

Afters

A Christmas Miscellany

Ingredients:
227 grams butter,
145 grams medium demerara sugar,
315 grams all-purpose flour,
pinch of salt.

Pre-heat oven to low heat (150° Centigrade or 300° Fahrenheit).

Cream butter and sugar. Mix flour and salt, and stir into the butter and sugar mix. Roll out to no more than a quarter inch (6mm) on a floured board (preferably a cloth-covered board). The biscuit will be crisper for being no thicker than this. Cut to any shape you wish, but cutting to a Christmas star shape will add to the crispness. Bake on un-greased baking sheet for 20 to 25 minutes.

'GINGER-BREAD COOKIES & STOLLEN' (RICHTER, 1861)

(iii) Almond Cookies

Ingredients:
227 grams butter,
100 grams sugar,
150 grams finely chopped almonds (from which the skins have not been removed),
2 tsp Vanilla extract (preferably Madagascar),
275 grams all-purpose flour.

Pre-heat oven to 175° Centigrade (350° Fahrenheit).

Cream butter and sugar, and stir in almonds and vanilla. Blend in flour (using, in order of preference: a pastry blender /two knives /a food processor /or your clean, floured, cool hands).

Take a bare teaspoonful of the mix, put on un-greased baking sheet, and flatten (quickest method is using heel of palm). Bake for 9 to 10 minutes or until lightly browned.

Makes about 6 dozen elegant, delicious almond cookies.

'SUITOR WITH A COOKIE'
['MIT 'NER BRETZEL...']
(L.RICHTER, LEIPZIG 1861)

(iv) Butter Cookies

I was given this recipe some years ago as a *Viennese butter cookie*, but an almost identical one appears (chocolate-covered) in the wonderful *Green & Black's Chocolate Recipes* as a *Breton butter biscuit*. Wherever it came from, it is a delicious, buttery biscuit.

(L.RICHTER, C.1860)

Chapter 14

Afters

A Christmas Miscellany

INGREDIENTS:
200 grams butter, chilled and diced,
375 grams plain flour,
150 grams caster sugar,
pinch of salt (if desired),
1 large egg, lightly beaten,
½ teaspoon vanilla extract.

Preheat oven to 160° Centigrade (325° Fahrenheit).

Mix flour and salt (if used), add the sugar and butter and rub between your fingertips until mixture resembles breadcrumbs (or process in a food processor).

Add the egg and the vanilla extract, and process again or mix with hands until mixture comes together in a firm dough. Wrap in greaseproof paper or PVC-free clingfilm and chill for at least 15 minutes.

Roll out on a floured board to about ⅛ inch (3^{mm}). Cut out biscuits with a round or shaped cutter. Bake on greased baking sheet for 15 to 20 minutes until a light golden brown.

If desired, dust the butter cookies with powdered sugar.

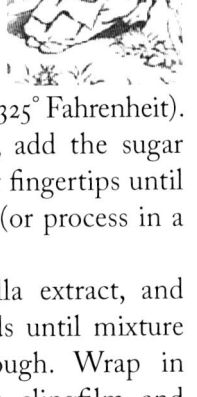

'ARRIVAL OF THE COOKIES'
(L.RICHTER, LEIPZIG, 1861)

3: Text of
A Visit from St Nicholas

THE POEM, *A Visit from Saint Nicholas*, by Henry Livingston Jr. (described and illustrated in Part I) has been republished many times, with several text variations.

The following is the text (and punctuation) as it was first published on 23rd December 1823 in the Troy *Sentinel*, New York State:

ACCOUNT OF A VISIT FROM ST. NICHOLAS.

'Twas the night before Christmas, when all thro' the house,
Not a creature was stirring, not even a mouse;
The stockings were hung by the chimney with care,
In hopes that St. Nicholas soon would be there;
The children were nestled all snug in their beds,
While visions of sugar plums danc'd in their heads,
And Mama in her 'kerchief, and I in my cap,
Had just settled our brains for a long winter's nap—
When out on the lawn there arose such a clatter,
I sprang from the bed to see what was the matter.
Away to the window I flew like a flash,
Tore open the shutters, and threw up the sash.
The moon on the breast of the new fallen snow,
Gave the lustre of mid-day to objects below;
When, what to my wondering eyes should appear,
But a miniature sleigh, and eight tiny rein-deer,
With a little old driver, so lively and quick,
I knew in a moment it must be St. Nick.
More rapid than eagles his coursers they came,
And he whistled, and shouted, and call'd them by name:
"Now! Dasher, now! Dancer, now! Prancer, and Vixen,
"On! Comet, on! Cupid, on! Dunder and Blixem;
"To the top of the porch! to the top of the wall!

"Now dash away! dash away! dash away all!"
As dry leaves before the wild hurricane fly,
When they meet with an obstacle, mount to the sky;
So up to the house-top the coursers they flew,
With the sleigh full of Toys—and St. Nicholas too:
And then in a twinkling, I heard on the roof
The prancing and pawing of each little hoof.
As I drew in my head, and was turning around,
Down the chimney St. Nicholas came with a bound:
He was dress'd all in fur, from his head to his foot,
And his clothes were all tarnish'd with ashes and soot;
A bundle of toys was flung on his back,
And he look'd like a peddler just opening his pack:
His eyes—how they twinkled! his dimples how merry,
His cheeks were like roses, his nose like a cherry;
His droll little mouth was drawn up like a bow,
And the beard of his chin was as white as the snow;
The stump of a pipe he held tight in his teeth,
And the smoke it encircled his head like a wreath.
He had a broad face, and a little round belly
That shook when he laugh'd, like a bowl full of jelly:
He was chubby and plump, a right jolly old elf,
And I laugh'd when I saw him in spite of myself;
A wink of his eye and a twist of his head
Soon gave me to know I had nothing to dread.
He spoke not a word, but went straight to his work,
And fill'd all the stockings; then turn'd with a jirk,
And laying his finger aside of his nose
And giving a nod, up the chimney he rose.
He sprung to his sleigh, to his team gave a whistle,
And away they all flew,
   like the down of a thistle:
But I heard him exclaim,
   ere he drove out of sight—
Happy Christmas to all,
   and to all a good night.

And to All—a Good Night

TEXT: *SENTINEL*, TROY, NEW YORK, 1823
(*WITH ORIGINAL PUNCTUATION & SPELLING*).
DRAWINGS: 1864, *PRANG & CO.*, BOSTON.

[*Note:* The original names (& early variations): Dunder
(/Donder) and Blixem (/Blixen), come from Dutch words.]

SOURCES

Principal Sources

Certain standard texts on the history of Christmas have been cited repeatedly throughout this book (by reference to the authors' surnames). Some notes describing these now-venerable texts are listed following.

'ALLES LIEST ALLES'
(H.J. BARTSCH, BERLIN, 1832)

1. Antiquates Vulgares, *or Antiquities of the Common People* by Henry BOURNE (Newcastle, 1725).

Henry Bourne (1694-1733) is among the most interesting and appealing of the authors relied on, not least because he was a true pioneer. An earnest clergyman and a natural, honest historian, he investigated not just old Christmas customs in his gem of a book, but every sort of ancient tradition (even the form used for exorcising a haunted house).

In his time, it was unusual for someone of Bourne's background to become a scholar, curate and historian. The son of a Newcastle tailor, he was expected to become a glazier, but was so academically gifted that he was sent to the Royal Free Grammar School and then won a scholarship to Cambridge. He was appointed curate of an Anglican Church in Newcastle in 1724 and died (under the age of 40) in 1733 leaving behind an unfinished (but impressive) history of Newcastle, which was published in 1736.

2. Observations on Popular Antiquities: including the whole of Mr Bourne's Antiquates Vulgares, with addenda to every chapter of that work: as also an Appendix Containing such Articles on the Subject, as have been omitted by that Author, by John BRAND (London, 1775 & 1810).

Sources

This book is a frightening example of what can happen to authors of great originality (after they are dead) at the hands of lesser writers.

Like Henry Bourne, John Brand (1744-1806) was from Newcastle and he too became a curate there. He does not seem to have shared Bourne's intellectual gifts—he was 28 when he matriculated to Oxford. In 1784 he became rector of a parish in London. In 1777, he had been appointed a Fellow of the Society of Antiquaries.

In 1775 (and again in 1810), Brand re-published the entirety of Bourne's book, adding to it footnotes that contained little in the way of new information but much criticism of the admirable Henry Bourne (as well as some interesting insights into Brand's own personality). Bourne, for instance, wrote a very interesting chapter on Saturday afternoon—how traditionally the Christian church had directed it was not to be part of the working week, but part of Sunday—i.e. Sunday's vigil or eve, and the time of preparation for it.

Bourne (as you might expect of a clergyman) regretted the loss of this tradition, of putting prayer before work on a Saturday afternoon:

> Never was man poorer for observing the duties of religion. If thou lose any Thing of the Wages of the Day, to do the service of God, he will take care to supply it ...
>
> ... Set apart this small time for the time of preparation.

The clergyman Brand took a very different view. After saying that 'Mr Bourne uses great affectation...' and 'He has printed the Latin erroneously too' goes on to criticise Bourne's attitude to Saturday afternoon as a time for prayer:

> Our author's Exhortation' [wrote Brand] ...is likely to misconstruction: An inference might easily be deduced from it in favour of idleness. Perhaps men who live by manual labour, or have families to support by it, cannot better spend their Saturday Afternoon, than in following the several callings, in which they have employed themselves on the preceding days of the week. Industry will be no bad preparation for the Sabbath.

3. *Observations on Popular Antiquities: chiefly Illustrating the Origin of Our Vulgar Customs, Ceremonies, and Superstitions, by John Brand, M.A., Fellow and Secretary of the Society of Antiquaries of London: arranged, revised, and greatly enlarged for this edition* by Sir Henry Ellis, K.H. F.R.S. Sec.S.A., &c., Principal Librarian of the British Museum; there were several editions of this book, the first in 1813; the references in this book are to the 1841 edition (Charles Knight & Co., London).

In this publication, Bourne's name has been banished entirely from the credits.

This useful book is different in arrangement from the earlier ones, and has much new information. What is impossible to understand though, is why Bourne's name was banished entirely from the credits for the book, even though Brand's book had, in fact, been Bourne's book, and Bourne's material is in it.

As to the material that did not come from Bourne (and there is a great deal of it) it is hard to know what came from Brand (in the form of notes, which Ellis put in order, and what came from Ellis himself). In any event, this is a well-organised, valuable book.

4. ***Christmas Carols Ancient and Modern with an Introduction and Notes*** by William SANDYS, F.S.A. (Richard Beckley, London, 1833); and
Christmastide, its History, Festivities and Carols by William SANDYS (John Russell Smith, London, 1852).

Sources

The Introduction to Sandys's 1833 book extended to 144 pages. At the end of it, he wrote:

> The Introduction is merely intended to supply any readers who are desirous of having a little insight into our old Christmas customs, with a slight account of them, without the trouble of referring to those numerous books to which I am myself indebted for the information. It is, what it professes to be, a compilation.

As a 'compilation,' the book could scarcely be more useful. William Sandys, F.S.A. (1792-1874), a noted antiquarian, ploughed through a vast number of dusty books and documents and extracted the Christmas-relevant passages. Most subsequent histories of Christmas made use of Sandys's research—including his own 1855 book which goes over much of the same ground. [When extracts from Sandys's works are quoted within the text, a volume reference is given only when (a) the particular extract appeared just in one volume, or (b) when the extract was relevant because of the decade in which it was published.]

5. ***The Book of Christmas; descriptive of the customs, ceremonies, traditions, superstitions, feeling, and festivities of The Christmas Season*** by Thomas K. HERVEY (William Spooner, London, 1836).

In this text, the wonderful illustrations by Robert SEYMOUR were produced first, and then the text was written. Much of the book is heavy going, and it could be better referenced, but useful information lurks within it. His citations from passages of stylish contemporaneous writers such as Leigh Hunt (following) are particularly useful.

6. *Leigh Hunt's London Journal* by Leigh HUNT (C. Knight, London, 1834).

7. *A Righte Merrie Christmasse* by John ASHTON (Leadenhall Press Ltd., London, & Charles Scribner's Sons, New York, 1894).

The following was what Ashton said in his Preface to the book:

> It is with a view of preserving the memory of Christmas that I have written this book. In it the reader will find its history, legends, folk-lore, customs and carols—in fact, an epitome of Old Christ-tide, forming a volume which it is hoped will be found full of interest.

Ashton usefully quotes original material at length.

8. *Christmas its Origin and Associations* by W. F. DAWSON (Elliot Stock, London, 1902).

A chronological history of Christmas.

9. *The Medieval Stage* by E. K. CHAMBERS (O.U.P., London, 1903).

10. *Christmas in Ritual and Tradition, Christian and Pagan* by Clement A. MILES (T. Fisher Unwin, London, 1912).

An easy-to-read, heartfelt history of Christmas by an author who has a good turn of phrase.

Sources

Illustrations

Date, author, and/or original source of the various illustrations are indicated in their captions. Many first appeared in various English, American or French illustrated magazines—the abbreviation *I.L.N.* stands for the *Illustrated London News*, *H.W.* for *Harper's Weekly*, and *H.M.* for *Harper's Monthly*. The 1869 *A Christmas Carol* illustrations by Sol Eytinge throughout chapter 5 were scanned by Philip V. Allingham and appear on *Victorian Web*.

(SANTA AND HIS WORKS, McLOUGHLIN BROS., 1896)

Libraries, Museums, Antiquarian Societies, etc.

Library of Trinity College, Dublin.

American Antiquarian Society, Worcester, Massachusetts.

Mount Vernon, Virginia.

Camden County Historical Society, New Jersey.

The Colonial Williamsburg Journal, Virginia.

Winterthur Museum, Garden and Library, Delaware.

Keeping Christmas Well

Medieval and Renaissance Drama in England, Vol 7, Leeds BARROLL, Editor (Associated University Presses Inc., New Jersey, London, Ontario, 1995).

Clavis Calendaria by John H. BRADY (London, 1812).

Iment.com, website of Mary S. VAN DEUSEN, descendant of Henry Livingston Jr.

Author Unknown by Don FOSTER (Henry Holt and Company New York, 2000).

The Road to Mobocracy: Popular Disorder in New York City 1763–1834 by Paul A. GILJE (The University of North Carolina Press, 1987).

The History of the Puritans by Daniel NEAL and Joshua TOULMIN (Bath, 1793).

Additional research by Frances Madden.

History of Western Civilization, A Handbook by William H. MCNEILL (The University of Chicago Press, 1969).

The Philadelphia Mummers: Building Community Through Play by Patricia Anne MASTERS (Temple University Press, 2007).

Christmas Mumming in Newfoundland, Essays in Anthropology, Folklore and History by R. Geoffrey STILES [eds.: Herbert Halpert and G. M. Story] (*American Anthropologist*, 1971).

Jane Austen: A Life by Claire TOMALIN (Viking, 1997).

NATIVITY, *BOOK OF HOURS*, NORTHERN FRANCE, 15th CENTURY
(DETAIL SHOWN IN COLOUR IN FRONTISPIECE)

Also from Phaeton Publishing Ltd.

The Secret of Jules and Josephine
—An Art Deco Fairy Tale
by Artemesia D'Ecca

400 pages, 22 drawings
ISBN (PBK): 9780955375620

Set in modern times and in 1927 France & U.S.

'...impressive and imaginative...'—*INIS* MAGAZINE

'...A wonderful book...it is for all ages...Irish fairies flying all over Opéra Paris...magic, time-travel, comedy, mystery...Irish fairies are the best!' —BRENTANO'S, PARIS

'...I think anyone who read her book would start believing in fairies. I've always believed in them. My favourite character was Fuchsia. I liked it very much...' —EMILY SCHOFIELD (AGE 11), MUNICH

'While sending a strong but subtle environmental message, the book evokes the swinging lifestyle of 1920s Paris, as well as life on board an ocean liner of the period, with a fair smattering of latter-day celebrities like F. Scott Fitzgerald, Charles Lindbergh, Charlie Chaplin, Coco Chanel and Sigmund Freud, who all help the fairies "at their time of greatest need."... It is all great fun, and cleverly done.' —*BOOKS IRELAND*

PHAETON PUBLISHING LTD. DUBLIN WWW·PHAETON·IE

Extremely Entertaining Short Stories
—Classic Works of a Master
by Stacy Aumonier

576 pages: biography, 29 stories, 1 essay
ISBNS (PBK): 9780955375637 (HBK): 9780955375651

Stories of World War I & the 1920s
in England & France

'Stacy Aumonier is one of the best short story writers of all time. His humour is sly and dry and frequent... And can't he write!' —JOHN GALSWORTHY (winner of the Nobel Prize for Literature).

'...a very elegant volume...short stories that invite comparison with those of Saki, O.Henry and even Guy de Maupassant.'—*BOOKS IRELAND*

BROADCAST ON BBC RADIO 4 *Afternoon Readings* in 2011.

'...in England, my first trip there in 25 years... I bought the new Phaeton collection of *Extremely Entertaining Short Stories* by Stacy Aumonier... greatly appreciated in his time for his wit and neatly contrived plots. Back now in New York, it's a heavy volume to cart back and forth as subway reading, but it's well worth the weight!' —*LIBRARY JOURNAL*, NEW YORK (2009)

'...a great holiday read.' —BRENTANO'S, PARIS

ALSO FROM PHAETON PUBLISHING LTD.

BRIGHTER FRENCH
—Colloquial & Idiomatic, for Bright Young People (who already know some) by Harry Thompson Russell
illustrated by Eric Fraser

336 pages, (incl. author's & illustrator's biographies)
20 drawings & 28 photos ISBN (PBK): 9780955375675
Volume I of the *Brighter French* Series

'Regarded as one of the best French language learning guides ever written.' —WILTSHIRE TIMES [2010]

1. 'What did he die of?'
—'Nobody knows.
But then nobody knew what he lived on, either.'

1. « *De quoi* est-il mort
—On ne sait pas.
D'ailleurs on ne savait non plus de quoi il vivait. »

'When did readers last read a really good dialogue in a language textbook with a real sense of conversation and a good punchline? For those with faltering school French, these books provide a breath of fresh air, quite a few laughs and some really useful idiomatic French...'—SYSTEM MAGAZINE [2010], ROBERT VANDERPLANK, DIRECTOR, LANGUAGE CENTRE, UNIVERSITY OF OXFORD

'Great Fun.' —BOOKS IRELAND [2010]

'...that brilliant volume *Brighter French*...'
—PREFACE TO TEACH YOURSELF FRENCH (36th impression, 1980)

PHAETON PUBLISHING LTD.   DUBLIN   WWW·PHAETON·IE

The BRIGHTER FRENCH WORD-BOOK
—A Guide to 'the Right Word' for Bright Young People
by Harry Thompson Russell

352 pages, 32 illustrations ISBN (PBK.): 9780955375699

Volume II in the classic *Brighter French* Series, written in the 1920s for 'Bright Young People who already know some'

'Great Fun.' —BOOKS IRELAND [2010]

Vocabulary on a wide range of subjects—both of universal interest : the House, the Town, Illness, the Weather, etc.—and more specialised : Horses, Firearms and Target Shooting, Finance and Business, Nautical Matters, etc.
—with distinctions that are hard to find in a dictionary.

'...remarkable for the amazing detail that is presented. The Motoring section would have come in handy many years ago when I broke down in France. ...Television and computers make no appearance, of course, but just about everything else is present in this handy paperback.'
—SYSTEM MAGAZINE [2010], ROBERT VANDERPLANK
DIRECTOR, LANGUAGE CENTRE, UNIVERSITY OF OXFORD